"I have known Herb Brown for many years, and his coaching philosophies and principles are second to none. *Let's Talk Defense!* will show you the way to establishing a superior defense, and it is a tool of the trade that both aspiring and veteran coaches should not be without."

—*John Calipari, Head Coach,*
University of Memphis

"Herb Brown understands the most fundamental aspect of the game and that is great defense wins championships. This book will explain the basic concepts of how it is done."

—*Joe Dumars, General Manager*
of the Detroit Pistons and
Six-Time NBA All-Star

"Defense has been a focal point for me throughout my career. Working closely with Herb Brown this year gave me an opportunity to work with a leading authority on the subject. *Let's Talk Defense!* captures the essence of his deep-rooted understanding of the way defense should be played, and I highly recommend it to coaches and players of all ages."

—*Lindsey Hunter,*
Ten-Year NBA Veteran

"*Let's Talk Defense!* is a comprehensive compilation of defensive schemes, concepts, and philosophies. It is the product of the Brown brothers' years of experience and leaves no defensive stone unturned. *Let's Talk Defense!* is a must read for both players and coaches at all levels of the game."

—*Isiah Thomas,*
NBA Hall of Fame Player,
Former NBA Head Coach,
and Current President of
the New York Knicks

LET'S TALK
DEFENSE!

TIPS, SKILLS, AND DRILLS FOR BETTER DEFENSIVE BASKETBALL

HERB BROWN

McGraw·Hill

New York   Chicago   San Francisco   Lisbon   London   Madrid   Mexico City
Milan   New Delhi   San Juan   Seoul   Singapore   Sydney   Toronto

Library of Congress Cataloging-in-Publication Data

Brown, Herb, 1936–
    Let's talk defense! : tips, skills, and drills for better defensive basketball / by Herb Brown.—1st ed.
       p.   cm.
    Includes index.
    ISBN 0-07-144169-7
    1. Basketball—Defense. I. Title.

  GV888.B76   2005
  796.332′2—dc22   2004019991

Also by Herb Brown:

Basketball's Box Offense
Basketball Coaches' Guide: Preparing for
    Special Situations

2 3 4 5 6 7 8 9 0 VLP/VLP 3 2 1 0 9 8 7 6

ISBN 0-07-144169-7

McGraw-Hill books are available at special quantity discounts to use as premiums and sales promotions, or for use in corporate training programs. For more information, please write to the Director of Special Sales, Professional Publishing, McGraw-Hill, Two Penn Plaza, New York, NY 10121-2298. Or contact your local bookstore.

This book is printed on acid-free paper.

Contents

Foreword

Herb Brown has been almost everywhere basketball is played. His coaching experiences have taken him all over the world over the past 40-something years. I know Herb has learned and tried to take something positive and useful from every stop on his coaching tour. The material for this book has been compiled from many different sources. I don't think you will find many coaches more committed than Herb Brown. He has always been a tireless worker with an unparalleled appetite for basketball knowledge. The man has dedicated a great deal of his life to the game of basketball and *Let's Talk Defense!* is just one of the fruits of his labor.

Herb and I have always believed defense to be the great equalizer. Even if your team seems short on personnel when compared to that of your opponents, a solid defense can effectively bridge the talent gap. Basketball is a basic game; if you score more points than your opponent, you win the game; and if you stop the other team from scoring points and play the right way, you can win games even when your team struggles offensively.

I think this book will provide players and coaches at all levels with a comprehensive and easy-to-understand blueprint of how to build a successful defense. We used many of these principles and techniques with the Detroit Pistons in the 2003–2004 NBA championship season. Success, defensive or otherwise, can only be achieved through hard work and dedication. Teams must be thoughtfully trained, drilled, and coached. Part of this equation for defensive success can be found in the pages that follow. The other parts of the equation will have to come from you.

I am proud of Herb's professional and personal achievements. This book is the product of his intellect, diligence, and vast experience in teaching and coaching the game of basketball. It's a tool no coach should be without.

—Larry Brown, Head Coach, Detroit Pistons

Preface

Defense is a state of mind. It is, in the opinion of this author and many other coaches, the great equalizer. Our philosophy has been developed over a period of time and it is being constantly refined to this day. This philosophy is not the only way to coach and teach defense, but it may give you ideas you will want to incorporate or think about adding to your own defensive philosophy. We all seek information that can help to broaden our horizons, and I hope some of these methods and ideas will help or encourage you to innovate and try different things.

Some of the material in this book may seem repetitive, but the repetition has been by design. Defensive mastery requires constant teaching, practice, and repetition. These elements cannot be overlooked if you want your team to be successful. There is also some overlap with certain tenets and principles appearing in several sections of the book. This is necessary to give the reader a complete view, in context, of each topic without confusing references to other sections of the book. Throughout there are pictures and more than 200 diagrams intended to help you visualize the movements and players involved in the various drills discussed. You will want to refer to the Player Movement Legend that follows as you study the diagrams.

It is my hope that this book whets your appetite and provides food for thought as you consider the importance of defensive basketball.

Player Movement Legend

PLAYER WITH BALL   ○

COACH WITH BALL   Ⓧ

DEFENSE x^1 x^2 x^3 x^4 x^5

OFFENSE   **1**   **2**   **3**   **4**   **5**

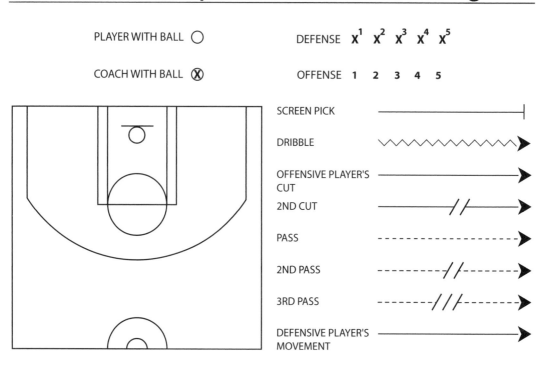

SCREEN PICK	
DRIBBLE	
OFFENSIVE PLAYER'S CUT	
2ND CUT	
PASS	
2ND PASS	
3RD PASS	
DEFENSIVE PLAYER'S MOVEMENT	

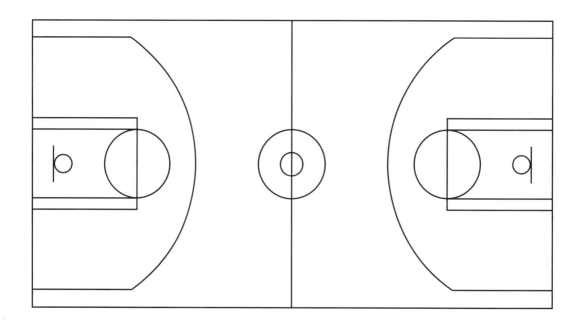

Acknowledgments

Writing a book on defense has always been on my agenda. I finally decided to put my thoughts on paper while I was an assistant coach with the Portland Trail Blazers during the 2002–2003 NBA season. Working daily on the manuscript, I was able to complete it while working as an assistant with the 2004 NBA Champion Detroit Pistons. It is my fondest desire that what follows will benefit the reader.

Many people deserve mention for encouraging and prodding me to complete this project, and they deserve special thanks. Without their assistance I might still be writing. I cannot thank the people at McGraw-Hill enough, especially my editor, Mark Weinstein, who believed in the project when I first presented it to him, worked diligently for its acceptance, and then continually provided ideas and suggestions as well as made certain that I met the necessary production deadlines. He has been a valuable sounding board as has been Heidi Bresnahan, my project editor at McGraw-Hill.

Thanks to the Detroit Pistons organization and directors of media relations, Kevin Grigg and Paul Hickey, for their editorial and photo acquisitions help. Thanks to Judy Dowgiert, Nancy Bontumasi, and Missy Erwin for manuscript and computer assistance. Thanks also go to Melissa Carbonaro for formatting the manuscript a number of times. Special kudos to Chris Hiller of the Palace Creative Group for his exceptional work on the book's diagrams.

I greatly appreciate the cooperation of the Detroit Pistons management—Bill Davidson, Oscar Feldman, Joe Dumars, and Larry Brown—and the finest group of NBA players and staff I have ever worked with, all of whom bent over backwards to try to make this book successful. The outstanding play-off performance of the Detroit Pistons reflects what I believe defense and teamwork are all about.

My agent, Matthew Brown, was instrumental in organizing and pulling everything together. He, along with Ed Krinsky and Michael Holton, provided many invaluable content and editorial suggestions.

I would like to thank all the coaches and players I have ever been associated with for their contributions as well as the many coaches and players who have shared their basketball knowledge, thoughts, and insights with me.

I'd also like to thank the players who played with me and the coaches who assisted me in the 1997 and 2001 Maccabiah Games.

A very special thank-you to my wife, Sherri, for putting up with my mood swings as I tried to meet my deadlines.

Defensive Coaching
Philosophy

When a team is prepared and committed to playing defense each time they hit the floor, that team has an opportunity to win any game, especially if they have dedicated themselves to *stopping* both the collective opposition *and* their individual opponents. Defense is a constant. It can help you win games even when your team is having an off night offensively. Defense is three-dimensional: it is desire, discipline, and dedication.

Your opponents may be more physically talented, but if you can limit their ability to score and take away the things they want to do you should be in a position to win just about any game. You must begin to teach and preach defense from the first moment you meet with your team. Just as you cannot wait to press until the end of a game when you are 20 points behind, you must immediately emphasize the importance of defending as the strategy to win ball games. Defense is not simply a last resort to get you back in the game; it is the solid foundation of a winning program. Defense requires discipline; if a coach is firm initially, he will set the tone early and never have to emphasize the importance of defense later on in the season.

Many coaches, most notably Hall of Fame coach Dean Smith, believe and have said, "Coaches are hired to teach execution; they are not hired to teach effort." Effort is the primary prerequisite for playing defense and basketball successfully. A defensive mind-set, effort, determination, and execution must be there every night in order to give your team a chance to win when the ball is not going in the basket and your team is struggling to score. Defense can change the tempo of the game and be disruptive. It can be used to force opponents into playing and executing against defensive schemes they have not worked with and are uncomfortable playing against. The aim of every great defensive team is to take something away from their opponents. Our goals are always to limit the opposition to one bad or ill-advised shot and no offensive rebounds.

Defense wins championships. This is true for most sports, not only basketball. Pat Summit, the successful University of Tennessee Women's Basketball coach, believes that "Defense wins games but rebounding wins championships." I tend to agree with her statement. However, our philosophy is still the same: Defense wins championships. We consider rebounding just one integral part of excellent defensive basketball.

Many times the crowd will underestimate or fail to recognize a team's great defense, but people in the know have nothing but admiration for these efforts. To develop a team's defensive attitude coaches must teach or preach defense from their team's first meeting or practice. The more frequently the players are reminded of the importance of defense and the more they practice and work at it, the more quickly they will understand how necessary it is to the team's overall success.

Placing an emphasis on strong defensive awareness and techniques is definitely not a deterrent to teaching offense. On the contrary, I have always thought it helps to make your team better offensively at the same time. Your team will get to practice against a defensive-minded opponent every day, and your defense is also forced to execute against every conceivable offensive maneuver they might face in a game. This will quickly help to enhance your team's overall offensive execution as well as each player's offensive abilities and skills. It will also help you, the coach, develop a multiple-offense philosophy. Face it, players love to play offense and they are always looking to improve their ability to score. Working against an aggressive defense every time they practice can only help the team's offensive execution.

The shot clock has also helped teams both offensively and defensively. The NBA, the minor leagues in the United States, and all of the international basketball leagues have adopted the 24-second shot clock, and it is my belief that this speeds up the game and makes players better and more skilled because they have to do things at a more rapid pace. I think colleges would benefit if they had the same shot clock as other levels of basketball. I believe high school and all other levels should continue to play with longer shot-clock time constraints.

It has always been my belief that you build a strong foundation first and then expand and develop what you teach. With that in mind I am a proponent of employing a varied defensive arsenal that includes many different schemes designed to exploit and keep opponents off balance. Today's coaches and athletes are so gifted that they are capable of scoring in many different ways, and you must have an alternate plan if one defensive scheme is unable to stop an opponent.

There is no one correct way to play defense and I will not pretend to present a defensive philosophy or strategy that is in any way original. My plan of action has evolved over participation in many basketball seasons. It has been and continues to be influenced by a number of outstanding coaches as well as by the changing nature of the game. In fact, I must emphasize that I am continually learning from coaches at all levels of the game. Many times when a coach asks me why we do something, explaining that he or she does it differently, it gives me pause and causes me to rethink the situation, which either reinforces or possibly refines my teaching of a particular defensive scheme.

My first taste of the importance of defense began when my high school coach, Bob Gersten at Long Beach High School in New York, emphasized man-to-man defense in all our practices. I can still vividly remember playing defense against a five-man weave, sliding through when the player I was guarding received the ball, and stepping back and letting my teammate through when the player I was guarding passed the ball to his teammate. I then continued to pick up bits and pieces of defensive strategy by talking to other coaches, working at basketball camps, attending basketball clinics, watching as many games as was humanly possible, and reading everything about basketball and defense that I could get my hands on.

Studying the philosophy, teaching techniques, practice, and game management of successful coaches has also continued to help me form a defensive system. I developed my first half-court defense coaching system after I'd viewed a soft-drink company's promotional film featuring Don Haskins and his NCAA Championship Texas Western University team. The film demonstrated the basics of their defensive system. I later learned that this was the foundation established by Haskins's college mentor, Mr. Henry Iba at Oklahoma State University. Iba's coaching and defensive philosophy have influenced many of the most successful basketball coaches of all time. He is the founder of one of the basic defensive systems of the modern game.

Certainly a great deal of my knowledge and success is due to the relationship I have had with my brother, Larry Brown, one of America's greatest coaches. As we were growing up we shared many thoughts about how basketball was and should be played, and fortunately we still are able to do so today. Having the opportunity to coach with him at the NBA level has also been a tremendous coaching experience in that we learn, perfect, and adjust our defensive techniques every day. He is a great student of the game and he constantly searches for ways to improve his team's defense.

Larry and I first learned about teaching and coaching from our high school football coach, Roy Ilowit, who brought us to camps in Maine and Pennsylvania, hired us as counselors, and had us teach basketball as well as other sports every day. He constantly tutored us by requiring that we teach fundamentals to our campers. The teaching of fundamentals on an everyday basis may now be a lost art, but it has always served us well.

I fondly remember the first book I ever read about basketball. It was a pocket book on basketball fundamentals written by Arnold "Red" Auerbach, the legendary former coach of the Boston Celtics. The book explained the basics of dribbling, passing, and ball handling; it stressed the right way to play the game. The book still occupies a prominent place on my desk. Red was my first coaching idol, and he remains a great influence on my career (even though I am not a cigar smoker).

There is more than one way to get the job done. So much depends on the type of team you are coaching and each player's unique abilities. You must get your players to understand that to play outstanding defense they must talk and communicate with each other on the court. Our defensive philosophy is based on our defense always taking something away from the offense. We always want to negate our opponent's strengths—and to expose and exploit their weaknesses.

As previously mentioned, you as a coach must establish rules for teaching defense, both for the team and for individual players. We think you should always emphasize putting pressure on the ball and having your hands up and active to contest all shots and passes. Different rules should be implemented depending on whether the dribble is alive or has been used up. If you believe in shrinking and clogging the middle and keeping it compact without applying extreme ball pressure, make sure you thoroughly explain and teach your system.

My brother's coaching credo, one I thoroughly embrace, demands that his players always respect the game and "play the right way." He requires his players to defend, rebound, run the floor, block shots, and constantly share the ball. He believes that everything else will take care of itself if his team concentrates on these fundamentals. We believe very strongly in these concepts and try to re-emphasize them whenever we address the team.

Different Coaching Philosophies

Great defense generates easy transition scoring opportunities and this makes the game fun. When discussing his basketball philosophy John Calipari, the highly successful University of Memphis coach, mentions that he wants his team to play aggressively and that he expects his team to commit at least 12 or 13 turnovers each game. However, he also wants his team to play aggressive defense by forcing opponents to have even *more* turnovers than his team. Turnovers are similar to poor shots in that they provide you with one less opportunity to score, but Calipari also wants to take at least 10 more shots than his opposition. He promotes aggressiveness. He doesn't want his players to play tentatively or scared on either end of the floor.

I've heard coaches talking about their offense. They mention how important it is to have their best player or players take the most shots. I believe this points out the importance of having your defense prepared to stop your opponent's key players by keeping the ball away from them as much as possible. Great offensive players instinctively know how to get the ball when they need to have it in their hands. Therefore it is crucial that good defensive teams work at denying great players the ball and limiting their touches.

A coach's defensive philosophy should be reflected in his or her defensive strategy and tactics.

Ours includes a preference, many times, for using some form of a full-court press after all made shots (field goals and free throws), following time-outs, after dead balls, and to begin quarters or halves. We feel it is easier to set up and/or change your defense in these situations. It also helps to eliminate confusion and indecision. I know a number of coaches who are not reluctant to go against the norm and change defenses on the fly in an attempt to unsettle their opponents. However, we don't feel that tactic meets our needs because we want each of our players to know what defense we are playing.

Goals of Our Defensive Philosophy

The primary goals of our defense are to always extend and pressure up the court to force the dribbler to turn and change direction, to body up and guard all cutters whether they be straight basket or weak-side cuts, to body up and go over weak-side flares, and to pressure the ball to prevent the skip passes, which help our opponents post the ball when we are fronting the post.

Another of our primary goals is to have our players always strive to make each other better. We must develop trust. We don't only require our big men to provide weak-side help defensively; we also require our guards and perimeter players to help on the weak side. When your team has shot blockers and great anticipators like Detroit's Ben Wallace and Rasheed Wallace, teammates have a tendency to try to steal the ball because they know Ben and Rasheed are back there to clean things up.

We do not encourage taking the easy way out, a mentality that we feel exemplifies losing basketball. Defense equals five men working together to stop an opponent.

Demands of Our Defensive Philosophy

Your defensive philosophy should be reflected by your defensive syste_____ _____ ____ _____ ____ team to play. The _____ _____ requirements our de_____ _____

1. We require o_____
defense after _____
ble. Many ti_____
decide to ch_____
pick up at th_____
instead as ar_____
and keeping _____
to use anyth_____
tempo and t_____
be indecisiv_____
aggressive o_____
sure up and _____
change defenses whenever we ____ __
necessary.

2. We emphasize playing great transition defense after all misses, steals, defensive rebounds, and turnovers. The first man back on defense protects the goal and his teammates hustle back and get level with the ball. We may retreat, looking for deflections, but we don't stop running to get level with or below the ball.

3. In defensive transition we continually emphasize the need to protect the goal, quickly change ends, locate and stop the ball, and get all defenders *level* with the ball. We discourage reaching or flailing at the ball in transition, a characteristic we believe fosters losing basketball.

4. Defenders should always exert maximum ball pressure and make all passers drivers if the dribble has not been used.

★ We encourage aggressive on-the-ball defense. Our objective is to control our opponents by stopping dribble penetration and a straight line drive to the basket.

★ Our players are taught to get their bodies up and into the passing lanes. We also make it a point to front or three-quarter all post players depending on the position of the ball and where the player is posting up on the court. We teach playing one half a man, bodying up and staying connected on drop isolations to prevent the spin lob. We must be aware of ball location and our opponent's position when deciding whether or not to front the post. When we front we want to bend down and sit on the offensive player's legs to deny him the ball and the easy high-low pass. We also want to body up and deny low post position, and try pushing the offensive player off and away from the low block.

★ We challenge and contest all shots. We always want our players to have a hand up to distract the shooter. We don't want to come forward and out of control when we close out. We prefer to give up a contested jump shot rather than a drive. Knowing the opposition's personnel helps you know the shooters you must challenge and stop and the shooters you want to allow perimeter shots. We close out long or short depending on the shooter's ability.

★ We always emphasize blocking out. We stress keeping our opponents off of the glass and try to limit second-shot opportunities. Our players learn to find the ball before they leave their feet to rebound. Effective defensive rebounding requires all five defensive players. Long shots equal long rebounds.

5. We want to establish and execute great help and support defense: we shadow, dig, and give full-bodied help; stop (prevent and limit) all penetration; and we shrink the court and pack the paint.

6. We orchestrate and develop weak-side rotation and help schemes (NBA Shadow or Tilt defensive principles), and we constantly emphasize the importance of not permitting our help to get beat.

   ★ We limit ball reversal, and we want to channel and/or influence the direction of the ball.

   ★ We decide whether we want to force the ball sideline or channel it toward the middle, and our decision may depend on whether or not we are blessed with shot-blocking presence.

7. We constantly stress the importance of defensive rebounding and try not to permit second shots.

   ★ Our players box out, pinch outstanding rebounders, and box the shooter on all free throws, and we require all five defenders to box out and look to rebound on *every* defensive possession.

   ★ We teach our players to tip out rebounds they cannot control by designating an area, possibly the corners, where we might want to tip the ball. Our players are then aware of where to expect the ball to be tipped. It's not a good idea to tip the ball long and start an opponent's fast break

8. We've developed half- and full-court zone and combination, man-to-man, match-up, or hybrid defenses. We feel you should have full-, three-quarter-, and half-court presses in your arsenal, each defense utilizing the

same fundamentals, rules, and principles but showing different alignments. These defenses are at your disposal should the game situation necessitate a defensive change. We also want to apply pressure and change defenses on out-of-bounds or dead-ball situations. You can decide, for example, if you want to surprise the offense by trapping the first wing pass over mid-court or perhaps double-teaming the first guard-to-guard pass in the offensive end of the court. Your objective should always be to keep the offense off balance.

Philosophy of Team Defense

Our goal is to have each of our players defend, rebound, run the floor, block shots, look for steals or deflections, and contest all passes and shots. If we can accomplish these tasks we know we will be hard to beat.

We expect to play hard, execute every night, work together, and demand of each other as a team. We practice hard to make playing the games easier. We must have our team prepared and accustomed to responding to pressure situations. This is a trait our players develop in practice.

When playing weak-side defense, the dribble or pass should always draw the weak-side defenders to the ball. They should be moving to shrink the floor as soon as the ball moves away from them in order to provide effective weak-side help; the dribble or pass should draw defenders to the ball to stop penetration and straight-line drives. The defenders off of the ball can shrink or clog the driving and passing lanes by establishing position to try to pick up an offensive foul on the player with the ball. It is imperative that your players understand the importance of making the offense throw an extra pass. Players should always move on the pass or dribble and not on the catch. They must move to help while the ball is in the air, not once it has been caught.

Whenever a defender picks up a charge or an offensive foul, it can demoralize an opponent and energize your defense. Team sacrifice and trust are what defense is about and we constantly remind our players that the little things win basketball games. Grabbing a key rebound in traffic, providing weakside help, rotating to pick up a free man, closing out and contesting a shot, pressuring or deflecting a pass, blocking a shot, fronting the post, or digging and doubling back on the ball are things that win games and enable teammates to have confidence and depend on one another. We constantly encourage our players to do these things and compliment them whenever they do things to make each other better.

For example, when defending against the double stack turnout, the defender on the ball should pressure the passer and then immediately jump back in the direction of the ball and clog the passing lane to stop the offensive player receiving the ball from penetrating and/or shooting. Again, he and every one of his defending teammates are always drawn to the ball.

Defending the low post when the offense overloads the strong side where the low post player is positioned is difficult to front because of the threat of a high-low lock-and-lob pass. We always try to body-up, stay connected, and play what we call "half a man" instead of fronting or three-quartering the post in this situation. We discourage the lob pass to the basket unless we are certain we have weak-side help.

Many different factors contribute to keeping your opponents confused and off balance. Your team must come out with a defensive mind-set at the beginning of each game, establish both tough physical and mental defense, and set the tone early. You can't be passive and then expect to turn up your intensity when the game is on the line. Be the aggres-

Jermaine O'Neal of the Indiana Pacers exhibits excellent help defense by rotating over to block Stephon Marbury's shot attempt.
Photo courtesy of NBA Entertainment.

Eduardo Najera of the Dallas Mavericks takes a charge from San Antonio's Tony Parker.

Photo courtesy of NBA Entertainment.

sor from the first jump ball and let both your opponents and the officials realize how you want the game to be played. Make everyone realize that your team's effort, intensity, and physical play will continue for the entire contest without letup.

Defensively, some teams believe very strongly on shrinking the floor to stop penetration and make the opposition shoot over them. Teams such as ours, however, believe that you extend your defense and pressure the ball as much as possible to make your opponents attempt things they don't normally do. Whichever system or tactic works for you is the best one. However, I honestly believe that if you have your players pick up full court and work to constantly pressure the opposition, and to harass and force the dribbler to turn and change direction, that you will develop better, more aggressive basketball players and defenders while also developing players who are capable of coming from behind to win games. You must always prepare yourself in advance to anticipate things that may happen during the course of a game or long season.

Much of our man-to-man defense incorporates zone principles when we are playing off of the ball or on the weak side of the court. We constantly make our players aware of their responsibility to help their buddies (the two defensive teammates nearest to them on either side) as much as possible. We want them to communicate, develop trust, and cover each other's back. As the old saying goes, there is no *I* in the word *team*—and defense is all about team.

Weak-Side Defense

When you teach and coach team defense and weak-side help, it is important for your players to understand they should never have their backs to the basketball. Repeatedly emphasize that if the dribble or pass is to draw them to the ball they must be able to *see* the ball. We want our players to react and move on the pass or dribble, not on the catch.

Explain, teach, demonstrate, and drill your weak-side rotations when the ball is thrown out of a post double-team. Your rotation depends on where and to whom the pass is thrown. We usually prefer the trapper to be the defensive man who rotates or runs out of the double-team. On a short pass to the near corner we may instruct the trapper facing the ball to rotate because he has a quicker and more direct path to the ball without first turning and pivoting.

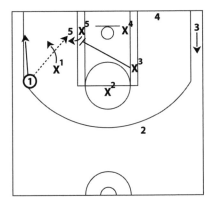

Figure 1.1
Trapping the post from weak-side high: cross-court pass from 5 to 3. Defensive number alongside X. Change in all directions.

Figure 1.2
Rotation on cross-court outlet pass to 3: X^2 rotates to 3 on the wing. Had pass been made to 3 in the corner, X^4 gets 3 and X^3 gets 4 unless X^5 is there first (see Figure 1.3).

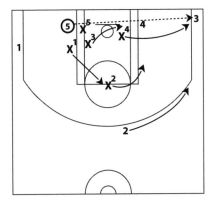

Figure 1.3
Rotation on pass cross court from 5 to 3.

2

Defensive Keys
to Victory

Basketball is a game of mistakes. The team that makes the fewest mistakes usually wins the game. This chapter emphasizes how to avoid defensive mistakes. Put the guidelines into effect during every practice and every game, which could result in huge improvements to your team.

Keys to Victory

Players must learn not to make the same mistake twice. As coaches, our job should be to point out and correct every mistake our players make. Try not to do this during the course of a practice scrimmage if it interrupts the flow of play, however. Permit players to learn how to overcome errors and to deal with adversity and changing game situations by continuing play. If errors happen repeatedly, you then have to stop practice and make your point. You can also deal with mistakes following the scrimmage when you critique individual and team performance or while you are working on half-court and transition situations in your practices. When you take the time to review or correct player errors, each of your players should be attentive. Impress upon them that what you are pointing out is the responsibility of each and every player on the team, not just the individual you are correcting. Any criticizing or correcting you do should not be personal. It is important for players to realize that they must listen to what is being said, not how it is being said. The message is what is important; players must learn to realize that correcting mistakes is a part of learning and improving.

We stress that practice does not make perfect but that perfect practice makes perfect. Winning basketball is achieved through practice and repetition. Your players must learn that correct execution is the result of constant practice, repetition, and drill. Your goal might be to make immediate corrections in practice in an effort to have your team react instinctively to pressure and a given situation. Instinctive reaction is best attained by creating situations in practice that enable your team to recognize, respond, and react automatically. We practice the same drills on a daily basis, emphasizing different looks and possibilities so that our players learn to react naturally and instinctively to various circumstances.

During shooting practices, develop and utilize drills that encourage your players to follow up every miss and successfully complete each shot or possession. This is not punishment. It is designed to make your players more aware of the importance of offensive rebounding, and it will also enable them to get off more shots in the same period of time. Successfully completing every field goal attempt might be the difference in your team winning a key game via an offensive rebound follow-up.

When correcting players or evaluating performance do so in a positive and constructive manner. Don't dwell on errors. Compliment your players when they correct mistakes and try to play the right way. Encourage them to raise the bar, and be sure to recognize their improvement and achievements. Make your players understand that if each of them is able to eliminate one mistake during a game your team has a much greater chance of being successful.

When making corrections it is a good idea to say one or two positive things to the players before you make your correction. I know educators who correct mistakes by using the sandwich theory. First they issue a compliment. Then they make a constructive criticism. They then end the discussion with another compliment. Everyone loves being complimented and if players know you recognize and appreciate the good things that they do they are much more apt to remain focused and realize that your criticisms are constructive and not personal.

You want your players to be confident; therefore you must always exude confidence. Prepare your players to meet any eventuality. When they go out on the floor they should do so with the knowledge that you have prepared them for any situation they might face. They must realize that they can adjust to and handle any situation. Repeatedly emphasize that they should be aware of time, score, and situation during every part of the game. They must also believe that you can help them by making adjustments on the fly during the game. Players must have trust in you just as they must develop trust in one another.

Remind your players that they must know or learn about an opponent's personnel. They must be aware of which opponents are scoring threats and what tricks they use to score. Your players should know when they should come to double-team or trap and which players they can leave alone when they dig or trap. Always try to vary and disguise your team's defensive looks. For instance, at times you might want to show a zone but actually play man to man.

Think about the kind of players you want playing for you. We prefer aggressive, highly competitive, athletic individuals—players who *act* instead of *reacting* to their opponents. We prefer players who make their opponents adjust to them. You can't always have the players you want but you can help develop and recognize your players' best traits and their unique abilities. Maximize players' individual strengths and minimize their weaknesses. Always try to put your players in situations that can help them succeed and perform to the best of their abilities. We never overlook a player who demonstrates a tremendous facility and desire to win. Players with high basketball IQs win games because they understand how to play and are willing to sacrifice, step up, and make game-winning plays and decisions under pressure.

Ask your players to help you establish and define your team goals. Break these goals down into your long- and short-term objectives for the team and individuals. Set realistic goals, but don't settle for less than you wish to accomplish. Dare your squad to overachieve. Have your players put their goals in writing and refer to them often, if possible, at least every five games. This will keep everyone on track. Discuss your team's goals for conference records, home and away victories, regular and conference championships, and tournaments.

We think it is a good idea to have our big men, wings, and point guards meet in separate groups before each game for two or three minutes to discuss what they want to accomplish that night. Encourage these groups to set goals that are realistic and attainable and make sure that every player understands his role, what each player's teammates should expect from him, and, just as important, what he should expect from each of his teammates.

Don't shy away from discussing why certain goals were not achieved. Your players should be more than ready to talk about how the team can improve and what each of them can do to contribute to the team's success. Encourage your players to be introspective. Have them verbalize their expectations and motivate and encourage them to strive to overachieve. Don't ever permit them to accept mediocrity.

Your practices should constantly stress fundamentals, team organization, preparation, and playing the right way. Don't take anything for granted. Pay attention to detail and try to anticipate and prepare for every possible situation. We feel it is your responsibility as a coach to get your players to understand the responsibilities of each position on the floor. Prepare them to react instinctively should they be forced to play another teammate's position. Instill in them the confidence and responsibility to be able to help the team in any way necessary. It is ideal if each of your players knows each player's responsibility on the court. Knowing what each of the other four players is supposed to do in any given situation will help the team perform more effectively. Confidence and poise breed success. Versatile and complete players usually earn more playing time and every coach should try to develop that type of player.

Prepare your team to execute and react instinctively under pressure. Explain, demonstrate, walk through, and practice. Drill at first without defense and then against a defense. Communicate. Take nothing for granted. Encourage your players and your assistant coaches to provide you with suggestions and feedback. Rely on them. They may notice something you have overlooked. Any information about your team or an opponent's weaknesses, strengths, and tendencies can help you win games and should be assimilated.

Try to plan everything you want to do or accomplish during the season. That's right: Plan the entire season. No detail should be too small. Decide what time practice begins, which locker room and lockers should be used, taping and taping order, stretching, pregame and prepractice routines, individual workouts, video, meetings, team dress, team travel, etc.

Rehearse your game-night activities. Inform your players as to the time they should be in the locker room, the time they should be dressed and ready for your pregame instructions, where their uniforms will be, your warm-up drills, bench decorum, dealing with officials, time-outs, halftime rituals, medical procedures, how to enter the game and report in at the scorer's table, how to handle victory and/or defeat, and how to deal with the media if that is appropriate to your situation. You can avoid a number of uncomfortable situations if you take the time to anticipate and prepare.

Prepare a player handbook that you can hand out at your first team meeting and be sure to review and discuss it with your players at that time. You cannot assume they will read and digest it on their own. Some will and some won't. Along with team rules and procedures, some things you might want to include are game and practice philosophy, team goals, offensive and defensive strategy and sets, important phone numbers, and team schedules.

This handbook will help you establish individual and team responsibility and accountability. Constantly review these rules to clarify, update, and go over any changes you might wish to make from one season to the next. If the handbook is a loose-leaf binder you might also update or make additions to the handbook as the season progresses. If you are coaching at the professional level you must include a description of the offenses that will result in fines, how much players must pay for each fine, the procedure for collecting fines, and the distribution of the fine money.

Meet regularly with your key players. I have always found it a good idea to meet with the point guards and the team captains on a regular basis throughout the season just as offensive coaches meet with quarterbacks and defensive coordinators meet with their middle linebackers in football. Here you have an opportunity to discuss defensive signal calling and strategy with the players who make the calls and implement your thinking. This also gives your players an opportunity to be integrally involved in your planning, tactics, and strategy. Direct your assistants to meet with other groups of team members to discuss specific assignments. Empower your coaches and players to contribute by establishing open lines of communication. Using this method on a regular basis will also help when you review each opponent's individual strengths and weaknesses as well as your specific game tactics.

Always emphasize conditioning. (See the Appendix, "Getting It Started: The Warm-Up" by Arnie Kander, Detroit Pistons strength and conditioning coach and physical therapist.) Your goal should be to have your team in better physical shape than your opponents. You want your team to be sharp but not overworked. It is a good idea to conclude practice with running and conditioning drills that have a purpose and are not construed as punishment. We believe in always using a basketball in our drills and in simulating game situations as much as possible. We emphasize focus and concentration and demand successful reaction and execution. We make our drills very competitive. We also believe it is a coach's responsibility to help teach players to react to and learn how to overcome fatigue and pressure.

Teams that are in superior physical condition tend to win. Well-conditioned teams are able to execute more precisely and effectively in the game's last two minutes. Our goal has always been to be the best-conditioned team, the team that can run all night without showing fatigue.

Shoot your free throws in pressure situations and set goals that have to be reached before concluding practice. Make certain your goals are almost always attainable and that your team doesn't consider them drudgery. Your players must relish the competitive aspect of the game. Teach them to learn how to win. You and your staff might want to consider working individually with selected players at the conclusion of each practice. Every player enjoys individual personal attention from the coaching staff, not only the starters.

Key Team-Defense Points to Emphasize

Use these defensive techniques to help your players work as a team.

1. Rebound defensively with all five players. Get every long rebound. Emphasize repeatedly that the longer the shot, the longer the rebound. If your opponents rebound offensively and consistently get second shots, they will beat you.

2. Your players should try to get better every possession in every practice and in every game. Effort and execution are not selective.

3. Your team should try to take something away from the opponents especially when defending half-court sets, early offense, and out-of-bounds plays.

4. On free throws make sure to pinch the opposition's key rebounder and box out the shooter.

5. You might want to zone or change defenses in dead-ball situations, depending on the time left on the shot clock.

6. If you have access to video and/or film, make it available to your players. Help them understand the benefits of watching video. It is part of their responsibility to utilize any and all resources that will help them improve their game. Video is a constructive tool and will help them become better players. The coaching staff should watch film and videotape with both the team and with individual players. Many players are more comfortable being critiqued individually when watching videotape.

7. When players switch defensively as two opponents cross with or without the ball, they must do so with the objective of trying to take something away from the opponents—for example, they must try to force them uphill and away from the goal to stop the ball, or each player must get back to his teammate's opponent once the ball has been passed. Do not permit players to run back to the player they were defending, leaving another player free.

8. Emphasize awareness of switching responsibilities when picking up a teammate's man in transition. Talk and let your teammate

The Detroit Pistons teams of the early 1990s were known for playing tremendous team defense. Here they are shown using their "Jordan Rules" to collapse on Michael Jordan.
Photo courtesy of NBA Entertainment.

know you have his man and that he must find your man or the free man in the direction of the help.

9. Your team should be aware of picking up early and applying defensive pressure after dead ball situations, made field goals, and made free throws.

10. Any time you can apply defensive pressure whether in the half- or full court you have an opportunity to disrupt your opponent.

11. Playing pressure defense is a tactic that will also help to get your team in great physical condition.

Defensive Keys to Victory

Encourage your team to keep the following principles in mind:

1. Out-rebound your opponents, and limit their second-shot opportunities. Box out!

2. Stop easy transition baskets and maintain defensive balance.

3. Stop fast-break opportunities by rebounding offensively and also by maintaining defensive balance.

4. Pressure the ball to get deflections and cause turnovers.

5. Generate great pressure on the ball when the dribble is used.

6. Take away what your opponents do best and force them to explore other options.

7. Try to eliminate and stop dribble and pass penetration.

8. Contest all shots by keeping a hand up to distract the shooter.

9. Make a quick transition from offense to defense.

10. Keep the ball in front of you at all times.

11. Make the rules work to your team's advantage.
12. Develop trust in your teammates.
13. Extend your defense and try to pressure and deny all entry passes.
14. We want our players to always be level with the ball and not trail the play.
15. Create havoc by moving your hands and feet to harass and force the opposition to adjust.

Additional Keys to Victory

Here are some more things for your players to keep in mind:

1. Emphasize out-rebounding the opposition on offense and defense.
2. Don't permit second shots and put-backs.
3. Stop easy transition baskets. Get back, stop, and see the ball. Maintain defensive floor balance. If your opponent's point guard penetrates, have your wings cover back; if a wing penetrates, have your point and the other wing cover back defensively.
4. Emphasize the importance of causing turnovers and getting deflections. Control the basketball and end up with more offensive possessions than the opposition.
5. Take away what your opponent does best. Don't give shooters an option. Force them to go one way when they want to use a screen.
6. Deny penetration and don't permit easy baskets.
7. Make the transition from offense to defense with all five players.
8. Get level with the ball. Keep the offense in front of you. Don't let anyone get behind you in transition. The first man back must

protect the goal and build the defense out from the paint.

9. Be in better physical condition than the opposition.

10. Make the rules work for you. Understand how to use them to your advantage.

11. Regularly make use of the shot and game clocks in your practice drills and preparation.

12. When you have a fast-break opportunity, the fifth player in the break must stay back and trail the play. You cannot let the defense get behind you in this instance because it may lead to a long pass and layup for the opposition. Keep the floor balanced defensively.

3

Coaches' Overview: Communication Between Players, Assistant Coaches, and Staff

Successful coaches strive to be responsible, dedicated, professional, consistent, and fair. Not only must they be outstanding teachers, but they also must have the confidence to create and carry out a successful plan. In addition, coaches must be flexible, tolerant, and willing to listen to new ideas. They must be able to think on the run and anticipate the changing situations within a game. Above all, coaches must possess strong leadership qualities. Players must trust that their coach has their best interests at heart.

Bill Russell, the great Boston Celtics Hall of Fame player, once summed up what we try to achieve: "Create unselfishness as the most important team characteristic." We subscribe to this mandate.

Once your players realize how much they need each other they will learn to play together and win together. Sacrificing and playing to your team's strengths form the foundation of a winning strategy.

Successful Coaching Traits

The following list was given to me many years ago by Stan Morrison, the former head coach of men's basketball at the University of Southern California. I have always strived to incorporate these qualities into my own coaching and teaching endeavors.

1. Industriousness
2. Enthusiasm
3. Judgment
4. Self-control
5. Earnestness
6. Patience
7. Attention to detail
8. Impartiality
9. Integrity
10. Teaching skills
11. Discipline
12. Floor planning and organization

13. Knowledge of the game
14. Professional physical appearance
15. Reliability
16. Optimism
17. Alertness
18. Adaptability
19. Intense desire for self-improvement

Here are some of my own additions:

20. Consistency
21. Concentration
22. Determination
23. Confidence
24. Empathy
25. Motivational skills
26. Delegation of responsibility
27. Interpersonal relationships
28. Personal responsibility
29. Importance of effort

Keep this list on hand. Review it, add to it, and upgrade it.

Coaching and Teaching Tips

As coaches we need to remember that players do not always learn, assimilate, and retain information in the same manner. Keeping this in mind is very important. Some players learn by watching, some by listening, some by visualizing, others when you demonstrate, and still others only by actually practicing through constant drills and repetition.

It's a good idea to be cautious when diagramming plays during time-outs; simply using *X*'s and *O*'s may not be clear enough. You may have to diagram plays using numbers by position or even by using a player's initials to make sure each player understands his assignment.

Sample Plays

The following are examples and diagrams of two plays an NBA team runs; the first is an isolation play that we will call drop one, and the second is a cross screen into a side pick and roll called either cross four get, cross four fist, or cross four out. We first diagram the play on the erasable board for our players to see and then we discuss how to defend these plays. Our discussion of how to defend these plays helps us to discern how our players learn once we begin asking them questions about the diagrams.

★ Drop one: One offensive variation of the common drop play (Figure 3.1).
★ Defending drop one by playing behind or fronting player 1 on the low post. If X^1 fronts 1, X^5 can look to double from across the free throw lane and weak and strong side elbows and weak-side box are defended by X^3, X^4, and X^2 (Figure 3.2).
★ The cross four get, cross four fist, or cross four out offensive play (Figure 3.3).

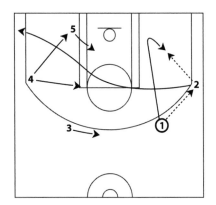

Figure 3.1
Drop one: one variation of the common drop play.

Figure 3.2
Defending drop one playing behind 1: if X^1 fronts, X^5 can look to double from across the lane and all other elbows and boxes are covered.

Figure 3.3
Cross four get; cross four fist; cross four out.

★ Cross four get defense frame 1: X^4 bodies up and forces 4 from low to high over the screen set by 1 (Figure 3.4).

★ Cross four get defense frame 2: X^3 forces 3 toward the middle and goes inside the screen set by 4 as X^4 either hard contact shows or zones up to let X^3 through. X^4 then recovers to pick up 4 rolling to the basket. The screener's defender can also body up and ride the screener low and out of bounds (Figure 3.5).

★ Cross four get defense frame 3: We decide to show hard or blitz (trap) the side pick and roll and then rotate big to big once X^4 has stopped the ball with X^5 crossing the lane and pre-rotating. X^4 dives into the lane once a pass is made and tries to help X^1 stop 5 driving into the paint. X^2 is ready to help stop 3's penetration and then recover to get back to 2. If 5 pops back instead of driving to the paint, X^4 runs and rotates to defend 5 and stop the pass from 3 to 5 (Figure 3.6).

Figure 3.4
Cross four get defense: X^4 forces 4 from low to high following cross screen by 1.

Figure 3.6
Cross four get defense: we rotate big to big and X^4 stops the ball. He then recovers into the lane to stop 5 driving into the paint. X^2 tries to help stop 3 and then recovers to get back to 2.

Figure 3.5
Cross four get defense: X^3 forces 3 toward middle and goes inside screen by 4 as X^4 zones up to let X^3 through. Then X^4 recovers to 4 rolling to the basket.

Areas of Staff and Team Organization

The following outline shows a team's organizational overview.

1. Pooling of resources and knowledge

   ★ Selecting a staff
   ★ Staff meetings

2. Discipline

   ★ Fun yes, horseplay no!
   ★ No sitting down (Have a meaningful plan for players who are injured or not participating in drills—for example, rehabilitation, etc.)
   ★ 100 percent concentration and attention during explanations
   ★ Consistency

3. Conditioning

   ★ Balance
   ★ Endurance
   ★ Adequate strength, muscle tone, and body fat
   ★ Avoid use as punishment

4. Daily mental preparation
5. Areas of emphasis

   ★ Team togetherness
   ★ Professionalism, style, and class
   ★ Representation of organizational pride
   ★ Give 100 percent every day

6. Practices

   ★ Interesting and competitive
   ★ Daily work in fundamentals
   ★ Attention to detail

7. Preparation

   ★ Special situations
   ★ Scouting reports and team and individual video sessions
   ★ Shootarounds
   ★ Scrimmages or exhibition games
   ★ Pregame
   ★ Travel Plans and Itinerary

8. Philosophy

   ★ Offensive
   ★ Defensive
   ★ Style (How do you want to play?)

Preseason Preparation

Preparation and attention to detail are the basis for a sound program. The following list is a sample. You can use it as a starting point. Organize and delegate these specific responsibilities to your coaching staff and administrative assistants. Never underestimate the importance of developing a strong foundation.

1. Travel procedures for away games
2. New rules from the NBA or your rules governing association: zone and eight-second backcourt rule
3. Scouting plans—team assignments for pregame presentations (exhibition and regular season)
4. Scouting your team (How many times during the season?)
5. New personnel—players and staff introductions
6. Video procedures and equipment—team and individual
7. Off-season—evaluation, draft, trades, free-agent camp, summer leagues, AAU, etc.

8. Individual workouts—selected players—conditioning, shooting, fundamentals
9. Preseason practices or training camp—location, duration, number of practices per day
10. Game day—shootaround procedures and pregame team meeting
11. Big-man drills; perimeter player drills
12. Stations—trapping, fronting the post, double-teaming
13. Strength, balance, and conditioning
14. Practice using the 24-second and game clocks
15. Special situations—last-second plays with and without the ball and when ahead, tied, or behind
16. Reading defenses

Working with Your Players and Your Coaching Staff

I attended a basketball clinic at which Isiah Thomas, president of the New York Knicks, made a presentation. His topic was dealing with superstar players and the individual attention and respect that such players warranted due to the tremendous pressure on them to perform at a high level every night. Isiah mentioned the need to confront issues head-on, but he also emphasized the importance of not embarrassing any player in front of his teammates and peers. He felt coaches should deal with difficult issues immediately—but always behind closed doors. Isiah also recognized that great players need freedom to help them override boredom. He declared that while you cannot treat all players the same way, you can and must treat them all with respect.

He made a point of saying how much he valued trust and how he believed in delegating responsibility and in having everyone know his philosophy. He stressed the importance of accountability. He mentioned that coaches must respect their assistants and get them to share the same vision. This makes sense; after all, if you trust your assistants you won't have to talk too much during practice. This improves your presence as head coach. Your assistants must bring energy to the floor each day.

Larry Brown wants to empower his assistants, not compartmentalize them. He prefers constant communication to encourage freedom of expression in meetings and on the practice floor. He rotates responsibilities, scouting, film work, and specific coaching assignments and encourages and stimulates openness and staff communication on a daily basis. His long-range hope is that eventually each of his assistants will move on to head coaching positions if they so desire.

Most outstanding coaches value trust and loyalty. They also believe in delegating responsibility. They know it's important for everyone to understand the team's philosophy and the importance of accountability. You should want your assistants to share the same vision you have. If you truly trust your assistants' abilities, you won't have to monopolize every practice with instructions. A head coach's authority is made clearer when his players realize that he values his assistants' input and contributions. Your assistants must bring energy to the floor each day; if they know you want and value their input, they are more apt to put forth great effort. A secure head coach treats people in the same manner that he would want to be treated if roles were reversed.

Good head coaches also encourage their assistants to meet with players in individual video review sessions. These meetings reinforce the respect the players have for your staff. The players become aware of how much you value and trust your assistants.

Qualities of Good Players and Teammates

Some people are naturally good members of a team; others must learn the communication skills to participate effectively. Here are some things individual players can do to improve as part of a team.

1. Always strive to make your teammates better players.
2. Play intelligently, play within the team framework, and display basketball street smarts.
3. Always think first about what is best for the team's success.
4. Try to act constructively during practices and games.
5. Always encourage your teammates.
6. Repeat calls and signals on the floor to help your teammates.
7. Be an active defender both on and off the ball. Deny and stop dribble penetration. See the ball when defending on the weak side and your man when defending on the ball side.
8. Concentrate, be focused, and react quickly and instinctively to changing situations.
9. Remain aware of time, score, and situation.
10. Limit turnovers and strive for at least a ratio of two assists for each lost ball.
11. Demonstrate good shot selection.
12. Shoot a high percentage.
13. Force the fast break but not the bad shot.
14. Work to become an outstanding free-throw shooter.
15. Do the necessary extra things to help your team win.
16. Rebound the ball. Make certain you know where the ball is going before you jump.
17. Retain your focus, concentration, and poise.

18. Be consistent and make intelligent basket-ball decisions.
19. Be supportive of your teammates and coaches.
20. Represent your team, school, or organization in a positive and respectful manner.

NBA greats Michael Jordan and Joe Dumars were like "coaches on the floor" and knew what it took to play championship-caliber basketball.
Photo courtesy of NBA Entertainment.

4

Defensive Checklist: Things to Teach and Stress Every Day

Our defense is determined to deter the weak-side duck in into the low post. We want to anticipate and beat the offensive player to the spot and ride him high or send him backdoor. This is best accomplished if we have suffocating pressure on the ball. We must use our hands to prevent uncontested passes and really smother the ball once the dribbler has picked it up.

Every part of our defense is designed to have our players act as a team, whether they are stopping ball reversal or getting back in transition to stop our opponent's early offense or fast break. Our defense runs to get back first, protect the goal, pick up free men, and stop the ball. If it becomes necessary for a player to pick up a teammate's opponent, he does so by talking to and communicating with his teammate on the court. We don't want to have two players pick up the same player in transition and let another offensive opponent get free for an open look at the basket. Communicating and talking as we retreat will help us accomplish this. Our ultimate goal is to limit our opponents to one bad shot on each possession.

Basic Rules of Defense

The following are rules we try to establish and emphasize to our players in every practice and meeting:

1. Stop dribble penetration. Control your man by keeping him in front of you. Keep pressure on the ball. Control and guard him one yard to either side.
2. Rebound defensively. Limit and/or eliminate offensive rebounds and second-shot putback attempts. Don't permit layups or easy baskets.
3. Deny easy transition baskets. Always maintain proper defensive floor balance. Defensive transition and quickly changing from offense to defense are major keys for stop-

ping a good transition team. Have your first defender get back into the paint to protect the goal and then build out when help arrives.

4. Always get level with the ball. This is especially important when your individual opponent trails the action. Get back in numbers and stop the offense from outnumbering your team in transition.

5. Deny penetrating entry passes and overplay your opponents. Force them to make the catch farther out on the perimeter.

6. Pressure all passers especially when the dribble is not live. Stop ball reversal. Don't let the opposition easily change sides or reverse the basketball.

7. Bump or chuck all cutters. Body up to them and ride them up and over screens. Don't give shooters or cutters an option. Force them to go only one way.

8. Slip screens. Don't allow yourself to be picked or screened. Try to slip the pick and go inside the screen or step in and pick up an offensive charge.

9. Front or three-quarter the post on the ball side. Force your man off of the block. The manner in which you defend him is dictated by whether or not the ball is above or below the free-throw line. Be prepared to have the defensive post man double the baseline drive whether or not he is fronting the low-post player. Don't hide behind the post player. Be ready to stop and trap the ball. We stress always fronting the low post.

10. Deny the high-low action on post feeds. Pressure the ball and the passer.

11. Double the baseline drive. We feel this is much easier to accomplish when you front the low post. However, it can also be accomplished by stepping out on the baseline side of the post man when you are playing behind him.

12. When trapping the ball force the passer to pass out over your outside shoulder. This enables the weak-side defenders to react and rotate. Emphasize to your players that they must seal the trap and stop or discourage penetrating passes. Read the eyes and position of the player being trapped to help you react to passes made out of the trap.

13. Take away your individual opponents' obvious strengths and deny them options.

14. Rotate to the free man in the direction of the help when leaving a trap.

15. Close out and contest all shots. Always keep a hand up to distract the shooter. Deny penetration by closing out under control and not running past the shooter. Be under control to guard against ball fakes when closing out on the shooter.

16. Don't permit personal fouls that lead to three-point plays. Make your opponent shoot two free throws instead. If you do foul, make your opponent earn his points from the free-throw line.

17. Always take ball fakes by first stepping back off of your back foot.

18. Make yourself long and wide. Get into the passing lanes. Keep your opponent away from your body where he is able to feel and seal you when he is receiving a pass.

19. Move on the pass, not on the catch. Move immediately in the direction of the pass once the ball is in the air.

20. Lock and trail on normal turnouts. Make your opponent curl the screen by getting on his hip and outside shoulder.

21. Decide to force your man one way on baseline screens. Get your butt to the baseline when defending post feeders and don't give them an opportunity to cut in either direction.

22. When defending turnouts off of the wide set play your man topside and force him away from the screen, or take a short cut and go through the screen rather than get on the offensive player's hip and outside shoulder to lock and trail him. Taking the shorter path is dictated by the position of the ball. The player defending the screener should not permit the screener to go down and set the screen. He must stand up the screener and then step back to allow his teammate to get through and make it difficult for the offensive player to receive the ball in a comfortable position.

23. Body up to your man and go over flare or jam screens.

24. Pick your opponent up in the backcourt and turn and force the dribbler to change direction as many times as possible.

25. Bump and stand up screeners.

26. Extend defensive pressure up the court. Pick your opponent up as early as possible. Work on disrupting his rhythm and concentration. Move your arms and feet to keep your opponent in front of you.

27. Force men without the ball backdoor, and then open up and retreat to the goal without losing sight of the basketball.

28. As an alternative to number 27 above, force players without the ball to go backdoor and snap back to defend the backdoor, clearout, or isolation plays.

29. Never lose sight of the ball. The ball should always draw and take you to your man.

30. Switch up the line if necessary on multiple and/or staggered screens. Do you want to go over the first and under the second screen?

31. Decide how you want your team to defend baseline cross screens. Do you want to step

To be a great player, one has to excel on both ends of the court. The 2003–2004 season's top rookies, LeBron James and Carmelo Anthony, understand that. Here the two square off, with Carmelo blocking LeBron's shot attempt with help from teammate Jon Barry.
Photo courtesy of NBA Entertainment.

up aggressively and force or deter the cutter away from his intended path or do you want to bump him up and go under on the baseline side? Do you want to force the screener low and ride him out of bounds?

32. Work daily on help and recover fundamentals to defend penetration and the draw-and-kick offensive maneuver.

33. Teach your players how to stunt, dig, and get back to their men.

34. Always emphasize *talking* and *communicating*.

35. Disrupt your opponent's offensive flow.

36. Use your hands to cause deflections as well as turnovers.

37. Concentrate on offensive rebounding to prevent leak-outs and fast breaks.

38. Maintain offensive floor balance to stop transition baskets.

39. Hard-trap and jump out when switching. Stop and turn your opponent uphill and back to his defender. Take something away.

40. In short-clock situations think about inverting and switching on out-of-bounds plays and switching whenever players cross or exchange positions in their half-court sets.

41. Hard-trap the point of the ball if your individual opponent is trailing the play up the court and you can pin him to the sideline. Come at the dribbler from a right angle in this type of trap.

42. When trapping, always try to turn the man with the ball uphill and back to his defender to force the player with the ball to pick up his dribble.

43. Think about incorporating and teaching NBA Shadow or Tilt defensive principles in your defensive schemes. Weak-side help is a must.

44. When playing off the ball, prevent dribble penetration by getting in the driving lanes

to help and recover by providing a full-bodied show rather than simply flailing your arms to try to steal the basketball. Force passes over your outside shoulder and look to pick up an offensive foul.

45. When helping a teammate in trouble it is always easier and faster to run forward to a spot in front of the ball instead of backpedaling to try to help your teammate. When teaching run-and-jump tactics or trapping, this is a good principle to explain and emphasize to your players.

46. When rebounding never jump until you know when and where the ball is likely to bounce.

47. When defending a high-post player with the ball on the perimeter, pressure up to him and play him as if his dribble has been used. Don't sag off and let him feed the post or reverse the ball to move the defense.

48. When defending a post feeder on the wing get your butt to the baseline and dictate where you want to send him on a cut to the basket. Don't give cutters a choice.

49. When defending the dribbler in the high pick and roll, play up and tough on the ball and you'll be able to fight over and not run into screens. Let the position of the ball dictate whether to go over or under this type of screen.

50. Don't permit players to make easy inside basket cuts. Drop two steps down and two steps in the direction of the ball every time a pass is made (jump to the ball and in the direction of the pass while the ball is in the air) to force the cutter to go away from the ball. The ball should always draw you to it when you're guarding a player off the ball or on the weak side of the court. Ride the cutter over or under the screen. Stay connected.

51. Stand up offensive big men in transition. Don't permit them to seal you and get the lane position they desire. Meet them early and don't let them get to a comfortable low post position.

52. Weak-side defenders should always know where the ball is; strong-side defenders should always know where their man is.

53. Rotate completely when the basketball is thrown out of a defensive trap or double team.

54. Always try to pick up the free man in the direction of the help.

55. Take away position on the post as well as the perimeter. Meet the post players early and stand them up.

56. Make big men (bigs) put the ball on the floor and dribble when they drive. Pressure them when they are used as passers.

57. Prohibit your defenders from chasing back pickers or screeners and screening their teammate defending the screen.

58. Body up to or butt-screen offensive players when defending against players using cross screens.

59. Trap hand backs and zone off of the ball.

60. Look to trap when the ball handler has his back to the other defenders. Always send the trapped offensive player back to his defender or uphill and away from the goal.

61. Always have five defensive rebounders. Long shots that are missed result in long rebounds, which the perimeter defenders must grab.

Vital Defensive Tips

1. You teach your team to switch on defense because you want them to steal the ball,

pick up the dribble, pick up an offensive foul, or take the opponent out of its planned offense. In other words, switch and take something away from the offense.

2. Your team can never be selective in effort and execution if they want to consistently win basketball games.

3. Defense is a combination of determination, trust, and communication.

4. You must take away your opponents' easy baskets and putbacks. Initiate and antici-pate; don't be passive and let the opposition dictate. Be the aggressor and make your opponents react to your aggressiveness.

5. The purpose of extending one's defense is to take things away from your opponent. Dis-rupt them and make them go to options they don't regularly practice. Stop the ball in transition before teams can initiate their early offense.

6. Stand up screeners and cutters to prevent easy catch-and-shoot scoring opportunities.

7. Referees won't take away your aggressive-ness if you defend with intensity from the beginning of the game. Once this is estab-lished, the physical nature of your defense will not be denied. Your goal is to take things away from your opponents and cause indecision. However, the refs may inadver-tently take away your aggressiveness if you play passive defense at the game's outset and only step up your intensity when your team is behind or the score is close. So set the tone immediately. Let both the opposition and the referees know early that you are going to really play hard, determined defense.

8. If your opponents are really adept at one part of the game you should think about countering their strength by using the same tactic against them. Many times their

Ben Wallace of the Detroit Pistons was named the NBA Defensive Player of the Year in 2002 and 2003. In 2002, he became only the fourth player in his-tory to lead the NBA in both blocked shots and rebounds in the same season. Here Ben blocks Milwaukee's Joe Smith's jumper.

Photo courtesy of NBA Entertainment.

In addition to his outstanding offensive statistics, New York Knicks legend Patrick Ewing also stands as the franchise's all-time leader in rebounds (10,759), steals (1,061), and blocked shots (2,758). Here he is pictured blocking the shot of Chicago's great Scottie Pippen.

Photo courtesy of NBA Entertainment.

strength may be also your opponent's Achilles' heel. If they press, then press them right back. Go for the jugular and exploit anything you think will help your team be successful. Disrupt whatever they have prepared for whenever possible. Keep them off guard and in unfamiliar territory. Take things away from them and make them have to adjust to the way your team plays.

9. Points to repeatedly emphasize: if you keep your opponents off the free-throw line, eliminate their fast-break layups, and prevent offensive rebounds that lead to second chance opportunities, your team has a great chance of winning any game.

10. Make sure your players are aware of time, score, and situation during every time-out.

11. When your team fronts the post or plays aggressive low-post defense you take away the offensive team's inside game and outlets. Fronting the post is most effective when the players guarding the ball put pressure on the passers, making it difficult for them to enter the ball. A low-post defender must also sit on the legs of the man he is guarding to move him off of the low block and stop him from jumping. When you front the post you must always provide weak-side help. Fronting the post is a tactic that takes things away from your opponents and forces them into uncomfortable situations.

5

Coaching Methods: Conducting Practices

As mentioned several times earlier in this book, our defensive rules demand that you must always see the ball and always be level with the ball and that you keep your man and the ball in front of you as much as possible. This chapter will show you how to conduct practices using techniques designed to give players the tools to enable them to stick to these simple rules.

Practice Philosophy

It is important that you not take for granted the fact that you have adequately covered a certain defensive tactic. You must constantly review your schemes to make sure there is no slippage. A team cannot afford breakdowns in the guts of a game because a player forgot an assignment that the coach hadn't reviewed or had the team practice.

We spend a great deal of time building our defense. We begin by playing one on one, then two on two, three on three, and four on four on both the half- and full court. At the start we do not permit switching but insist that our players fight through screens by talking and helping one another. We want to control and slow down our opponent's advance up the court by pressuring and constantly making the dribbler change direction with the ball.

We make our drills as competitive as possible. Many times we will place a limit on the number of dribbles a player or group may use to advance the ball; at other times we permit the players to freelance and play on their own. In practice we want the offense to try and beat our defense as efficiently and quickly as possible as our defense works to prevent this from happening.

We try to re-create actual game situations in our practices. We accomplish this by breaking down individual offensive schemes and practicing two-, three-, four-, and five-man situations. We practice against all of these situations on the half-court and our two-, three-, four-, and five-player pressure defenses on both the three-quarter and full court. There are many different basketball situations that occur when one team has a numbers advantage and we try to simulate and practice against these combinations. Much of our practice time is devoted to breaking down actual game situations so we can learn to defend them. *We love to extend our defense and pick up opponents early.*

We try to utilize the shot and game clocks in our drills. This enables our players to practice in a more realistic environment, which helps them become more aware of the time, score, and situation. They learn to react spontaneously to different pressure situations and become more accustomed to playing under pressure.

Building Your Defense in Practice

There are some drills you might want to consider incorporating into your daily preseason practices. This section will describe some of these drills with diagrams. Many of the drills can be used on both the full court and half-court. We suggest you begin drilling on the full court if you feel you have personnel that will enable you to pressure and extend your defense. Even if your personnel doesn't warrant it we think practicing and pressing full court will make your players better and also help your team's conditioning process.

Defensive Slide and Change-of-Direction Drill. Space seven chairs or cones on the full court as shown in Figure 5.1. Line up your players in a defensive stance facing the nearest goal with each defender guarding an imaginary offensive player. Each defensive player slides with his knees bent, staying low, and moves laterally until reaching a cone or chair on the court. Once there, he pivots and changes direc-

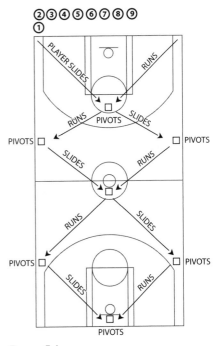

Figure 5.1
Cone or chair drill.

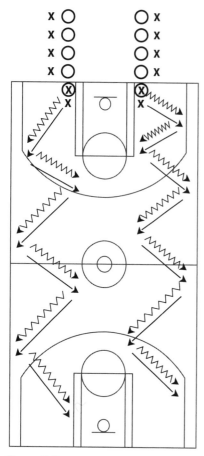

Figure 5.2
One-against-one zigzag drill.

tion and quickly sprints to the next cone. There he continues to maintain a low center of gravity, pivots, changes direction, and slides to the next cone. He then alternates each run-and-slide sequence, changing direction until he reaches the opposite baseline. We have our players repeat this drill four or five times to teach them how to slide to keep an opponent in front of them and how to run and pivot, release and catch up to, and turn a quicker opponent. A coach or manager should be stationed at each cone or chair to make sure the players run, slide, and pivot correctly. The next player does not begin until the player in front of him reaches the first cone.

One-Against-One Zigzag Drill. We run this drill first without and then with the basketball. It teaches the defender how to keep the dribbler in front of him and to make the dribbler use a crossover dribble to change direction. The defender must then get to a spot in front of the dribbler's outside hand to make him again change direction as many times as possible before reaching the far baseline. Players then change from offense to defense and repeat the drill going the other way.

Two-Against-Two Full Court. A coach or player initiates the drill with a pass and two defenders play two offensive players. As shown in Figure 5.3,

Figure 5.3
X¹ slides back to permit X² through on the DHO.

Figure 5.4
X² runs and jumps 1 as X¹ runs to defend 2.

defenders slide through on a pass or dribble handoff and try to turn the dribbler by pressuring the ball. Following a few repetitions we begin to trap the dribble handoff or run and jump at the dribbler as the defenders switch. The offense can either pass and split the defenders or pass and pick the point of the ball. We do not allow the offense to throw a long pass. We are playing two against two in this drill with no defensive players back to provide help to guard against a backdoor cut.

On the pass from out of bounds to player 1, player X^2 jumps in the direction of the pass in the middle of a *V* to see both man and ball and to prepare to fake at the ball to stop penetration. Each time a pass is made or a player dribbles away, the defender off of the ball must be drawn toward it to be in a help-and-recover defensive position. This is shown in Figure 5.4.

As player 1 receives the ball, defender X^2 slides through on the dribble exchange between offensive players 1 and 2. You can see this action in Figure 5.5.

Full Court with Three Against Two. Figure 5.6 shows X^1 jumping to the ball on the pass from 2 to 1 with X^2 helping and following 2 as he attempts to split the defenders and open up the court for X^1. This is a full-court drill with two defenders trying to contain and keep three offensive players in front of them

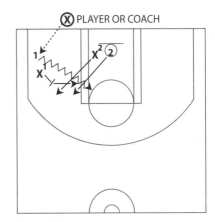

Figure 5.5
Two-against-two full-court drill with a pass from out of bounds: X^1 slides in front of X^2 to get in position to control 1.

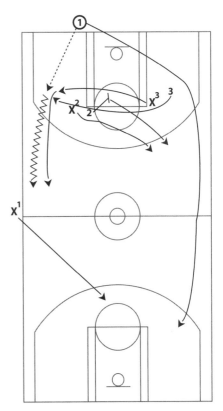

Figure 5.6
Full court: three offensive players against two defenders plus trailer.

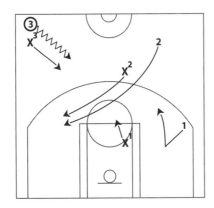

Figure 5.7
X^2 is in a position to take away the pass to 2 or run and jump or trap 3.

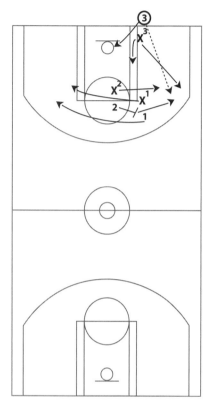

Figure 5.8

Three-against-three full-court drill—
player inbounds: X³ may pressure ball
or drop and help X¹ and X² defend
against the first pass and then double
the entry.

Figure 5.9

Three-against-three full-court drill—
coach inbounds: coach may pass to any
one of three offensive players.

until a trailing teammate arrives to help. In Figure 5.7, we add the third defender from mid-court sideline once the ball has passed half-court. The players then play three against three in the front court until a score or stop.

Three-Against-Three Full-Court Drill. In the drill shown in Figure 5.8, the emphasis is on containing the offense by talking and helping each other through on-dribble exchanges, player exchanges, or screens on the weak side of the court. Weak-side or help-side defenders must be drawn to the ball. Player 3 makes the initial inbounds pass against pressure.

In a variation of the preceding drill, in Figure 5.9 a coach inbounds and defenders play three against three using all offensive and defensive options.

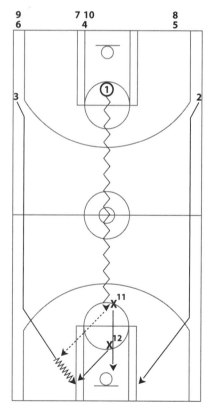

Figure 5.10

Three-against-two continuous full-court fast-break drill: in a tandem defense the back defender takes first pass.

Figure 5.10 shows a three-against-two, two-against-one, one-against-one, continuous full-court fast-break drill.

In Figure 5.11 the two retreating defenders play tandem defense with bottom defender guarding the first attempted scoring pass to the wing. Figure 5.11 then shows one defender retreating and keeping the two offensive players in front of him to contain, slow, or stop the fast break until defensive help arrives.

In Figure 5.12 we see one defender using full-court pressure to force the dribbler to continually change direction.

Figure 5.13 shows one against one in a front-court defensive drill where the defender forces the dribbler toward the sideline to keep the ball out of the middle.

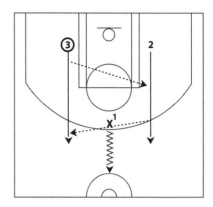

Figure 5.11
Two-against-one full-court drill: X¹ must retreat contain to keep ball in front of him as he retreats to the goal.

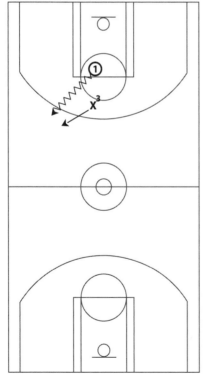

Figure 5.12
One-against-one full-court drill: we want to keep the dribbler down the sideline and out of the middle once the ball crosses midcourt.

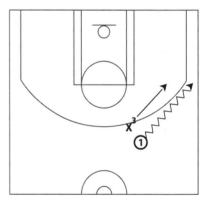

Figure 5.13
One against one in half-court.

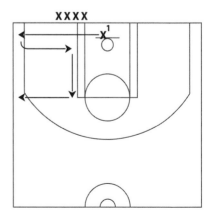

Figure 5.14
Defensive slide, backpedal, pivot, and run.

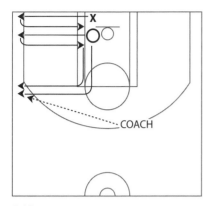

5.15
Slide mirror drill with coach passing ball to offensive player.

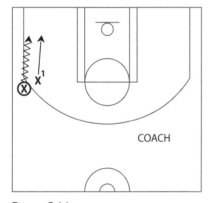

Figure 5.16
One on one after coach passes the ball.

Defensive Slide, Backpedal, Pivot, and Run. Figure 5.14 shows how one defensive player faces the baseline and slides across the court to the sideline, then slides back to the low block, backpedals to the foul line, pivots, and runs to the foul line extended.

Figure 5.15 shows what happens if you add an offensive player to the previous drill. The offensive player faces the baseline and the defender, where they mirror each other and slide, backpedal, pivot, and run to the wing area at the foul line extended.

In Figure 5.16 after the coach drops a loose ball for the offensive player to pick up, the two players play one against one.

One-on-One Post Defense Beginning with Three-Quartering and Then Stepping in Front of the Post. Three passers, one offensive post player, and a post defender attempt to front or three-quarter the low post in relation to the ball. The post defender steps across with his inside foot to front and sits on the legs of the offensive player as the ball is passed from P[1] to P[2] and P[3] while X then three-quarters the post once again. The defender sits on the legs of the player he is guarding to stop the offensive player from jumping (Figure 5.17).

Figure 5.17
Post defense general rule: play three-quarter with ball in the corner or on top. Front with ball on the wing. Three-quarter or front with the ball at the top.

Figure 5.18
Pass to the post with feeder as a cutter.

Two-on-Two Post Defense with the Passer Cutting or Spotting Up. For the play in Figure 5.18, the entry pass is thrown to the post from the wing. The passer's defender first pressures the ball; when the pass is thrown he then drops level with the ball with his butt to the baseline to force the cutter to go up the middle toward the defensive help rather than toward the baseline.

As shown in Figure 5.19, the feeder's defender is level with the ball with his butt to the baseline; the cutter now can only cut toward the middle as we have taken away the option to cut either way. We can also sag toward the middle to force the cutter sideline if we feel this is our best defensive option.

Three-Against-Three Continuous Full-Court Drill. We begin by playing three against three on the half-court. The three defensive players then rotate and play full-court offense against three new defensive players who are waiting for them as they cross half-court (as shown in Figure 5.20). We keep repeating the process with three new defensive players rotating up to half-court to meet the group of players who have just changed from defense to offense. We run this transition defense drill for 8 to 12 minutes with the constant rotation of players.

Four-Against-Four Full-Court Continuous Full-Court Drill. This is the same as our three-against-three continuous full-court drill. We will also run this drill using five against five.

Two-Against-Two Half-Court from the Top of the Key and Wing. As shown in Figure 5.21, we play two against two from the point and the wing, from a two-guard front, the pinch post, and the wing and low post. We practice defending each of our passing and cutting schemes at our defensive stations.

X^3 tries to get ball-you-man to deny 3 the ball, and force him backdoor or pressure him into catch-

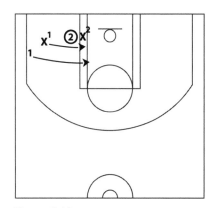

Figure 5.19
Cutter's defender with butt to baseline forcing cut to the middle.

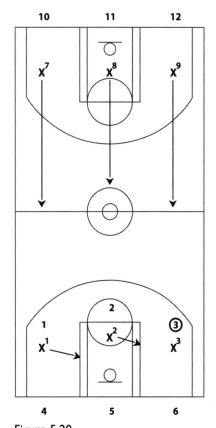

Figure 5.20
Three-against-three continuous fast-break drill.

Figure 5.21
Two against two from wing and paint.

Figure 5.22
Point-to-corner pass and cut: pressure the pass and then take away the inside cut.

ing the ball out on the floor and away from the basket. Once 3 receives the ball, X³ pressures him uphill and away from the goal. On the pass from 1 to 3, X¹ takes two steps down and two steps in the direction of the pass to take away 1's inside cut and post-up. We vary the pass and cut to set up different scenarios as we learn to defend on the half-court.

Defending the give-and-go maneuver from the corner pass and cut is shown in Figure 5.22.

Three-Against-Three Half-Court Drill. This is the strategy for defending the jam or back screen and flare. As shown in Figure 5.23, X¹ bodies up to force 1 over the top of the screen while X⁴ hesitates, stays attached to stop the slip by 4 and helps until X¹ has recovered to his opponent. We can then set up any number of different three-player situations to defend. Many offensive plays in basketball involve two or three players, and your team must learn how to defend these plays. For example, 4 may go and re-screen 1 as X⁴ helps when X¹ tries to get over the screen.

In Figure 5.24, we have three against three defending the pass and screen away.

Figure 5.25 shows three against three weak-side help defense with X² defending a baseline drive by X³.

Figure 5.23
Defending the jam or the back-screen flare.

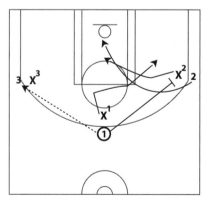

Figure 5.24
Three-against-three pass and screen away.

Four-on-Four Half-Court Shell Support Drill. Our defenders move on the pass (every two seconds) and are drawn to the ball while it is in the air. We teach our weak-side defenders to stay in line with the ball and the basket to help stop dribble penetration. This drill is illustrated in Figure 5.26.

Two-Against-Two Screening Drill with Coach as Passer. In Figure 5.27, we see a two-on-two half-court defense in which a coach serves as a passer. Player 2 throws a return pass to the coach and cuts off of a screen set by 3. Then X^3 must call out the screen letting X^2 know that it is coming. This permits X^2 to cut in front of him to defend 2. The coach is always available as an outlet for the players so they can continually pass and screen away. We play until a score or a defensive stop; then rotate from offense to defense.

Three-Against-Three Half-Court Screening/Cutting Drill. This is the same drill as the one shown in Figure 5.27 except that we now screen and cut three against three with the coach as a passer and outlet receiver (Figure 5.28).

Half-Court Shell Drill. This defense uses four on four on four (12 players and three teams). A team can only score by getting defensive stops. You can

Figure 5.25
Three-against-three weak-side help and rotation versus the baseline drive.

Figure 5.26
Shell defense four-against-four support drill.

Figure 5.28
Three-against-three screening drill with coach as a passer and an outlet.

Figure 5.27
Two-against-two screening drill with coach as a passer and an outlet.

Figure 5.29
Shell drill: guard-to-guard entry with a weak-side guard-to-forward exchange. X¹ steps back and lets X³ slide in front of him to defend 3.

Figure 5.30
Guard-to-forward pass with guards interchanging.

also have a team remain on defense as long as they continue to get stops or you can make the defensive team get two or three stops in succession. If you give up an offensive rebound, you lose a stop even if you subsequently do not give up a basket on that entire possession. Keeping your opponent from getting offensive rebounds is a key component to playing good defense. We rebound with all four defensive players in this drill. We believe that this drill should be used almost daily throughout the season.

This drill teaches players many things about how to play great man-to-man defense. First it teaches players to help their teammates. It also reinforces the idea that the dribble or the pass always has to draw weak-side defenders toward the ball.

We break the drill down into the following segments for teaching purposes before playing our game of stops. We constantly practice and review these fundamentals throughout the season.

1. Support (see Figure 5.26). The ball is passed over the head every two seconds to teach players to move on the catch, not on the pass, and to always be level and even with the ball and the basket on the weak side.

Figure 5.31
Guard-to-forward entry with strong-side guard cutting opposite and receiving a weak-side pin down.

2. Guard-to-guard entry pass with a weak-side guard-to-forward exchange. Here 1's dribble is live and therefore X^2 is in a help (rather than a deny) position (Figure 5.29).

3. On a guard-to-forward entry pass, the strong-side guard screens away and exchanges with the weak-side guard (Figure 5.30). On the weak-side down screen, X^1 steps back and lets X^3 slide in front of him on the guard-to-forward interchange.

4. A guard-to-forward entry pass with the strong-side guard cutting through to the opposite wing while the weak-side guard replaces to swing the ball. The weak-side forward pins down for the original passer as the ball is reversed, as shown in Figure 5.31. X^1 slides up and through screen set by 4 because the ball is on the other side of the imaginary dotted line through the center of the court and he is in a help position. If 2 had the ball, X^1 would lock and trail on 1's hip and outside shoulder since X^1 is one pass away from the ball.

5. Next we have a guard-to-forward entry pass with the guard burying in the strong side corner to set up a slice cut by the strong side wing as the ball is reversed. This is shown in Figure 5.32. X^1 follows 1 to the corner after getting level with the ball on the first pass. On the return pass from 3 to 1, X^3 steps to the ball, riding and taking away 3's inside cut as X^2 and X^4 are drawn to the ball to provide weak-side help.

6. A guard-to-forward entry pass with the strong-side guard, 1, burying in the strong-side corner as the strong-side wing, 3, passes to the weak-side forward, 4, flashing to the pinch post to play two-man action with the weak-side guard, 2, as shown in Figure 5.33. X^4 must call out the pinch post

Figures 5.32
Guard-to-forward entry pass with guard burying in strong-side corner. Weak-side help is drawn to the ball.

Figure 5.33
Guard-to-forward entry with blind pig flash post action.

Figure 5.34
Guard-to-forward entry with strong-side guard setting a cross screen for the weak-side forward.

Figure 5.35
Guard-to-forward handback entry with weak-side forward slicing to the strong-side post.

flash and permit X^2 to slide through or go below 4 to get to 2. If 3 has the ball and 4 sets a flare screen for 2, X^2 fights over the screen as X^4 helps and prevents 4 from slipping to the basket. We can also predetermine that we will trap with X^2 and X^4 on this pinch post action.

7. On a guard-to-forward entry pass, the strong-side guard sets a low cross screen for the weak-side forward to cross the lane and post up as shown in Figure 5.34. We want X^4 to body up to 4 to force him from low to high. X^1 follows the screener, 1, and provides help by slowing up 4 on the cut to the low post or he can ride 1 out of bounds to stop him from screening. We can then set a guard-to-guard pick-the-picker screen action with 2 screening down for 1. X^2 would then try to stand 2 up and let X^1 through or we might decide to have X^2 and X^1 switch this maneuver.

8. Guard-to-forward entry pass and hand back and slice cut by strong-side forward (Figure 5.35). X^3 steps back and lets X^1 slide through to cover 1 or X^3 and X^1 can switch or trap the hand back. When X^1 slides

Figure 5.36
Help and recover stopping dribble drive penetration between two defenders.

through, X⁴ bodies up to 4 and forces him low to high on his cut. If X⁴ can beat 4 across the lane on the low post, we want him to front 4 with X¹ pressuring the passer.

9. A help and recover dribble entry to stop dribble penetration is shown in Figure 5.36. We begin this drill by having each of our perimeter players drive between two defenders, forcing them to close out and stop dribble penetration and draw and kick options. The diagram in Figure 5.37 shows how we want to rotate to double the baseline drive. 4 drives baseline and beats X³. When X³, who has been drawn to the ball on the dribble, recognizes this he crosses the lane from the weak side to stop and double-team 4 with X⁴. Weak-side defenders X¹ and X² rotate back clockwise to protect the basket (box) and the foul line and lane (plug or nail position).

10. Figure 5.38 features a guard-to-forward dribble out entry with the weak-side forward coming across the lane to the foul line extended to set up a wing screen and roll with the strong-side guard. X⁴ follows 4 across the floor and contact shows to stop 1 from penetrating the middle on the pick and roll as X¹ fights over the screen. X⁴ must recover to the screener unless we have decided to prerotate big to big on the wing pick and roll.

11. In Figure 5.39 we have a guard-to-forward dribble handoff (DHO) with weak-side guard-to-forward exchange. X¹ must step back and let X³ slide in front of him on the dribble exchange between 1 and 3. On the weak side, X² must step back and let X⁴ slide through on the interchange. We practice defending this maneuver because many

Figure 5.37
Rotating and double-teaming to defend the baseline drive.

Figure 5.38
Guard-to-forward dribble out entry and wing pick and roll with opposite forward or center.

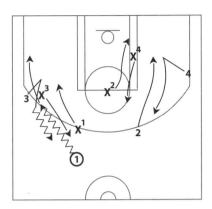

5.39
Strong-side guard-to-forward dribble handoff with weak-side guard-to-forward exchange.

Figure 5.40
Guard-to-guard entry pass with passer cutting to opposite baseline: X^1 takes away the inside cut by 1.

teams now use the offensive dribble hand-off exchange as a prelude to slicing the forward across the lane as the ball is reversed. Our forwards learn to defend a cut from this area of the court after the offensive player makes his pass. The defender tries not to let the weak-side cutter cut in front of his face.

12. Figure 5.40 shows a guard-to-guard entry pass with the passer cutting diagonally through the lane to the opposite baseline. X^1 must move on the pass from 1 to 2 and be prepared to cover 1 on the cut from the weak to the strong side as the ball is passed from 2 to 4. This maneuver of cutting a guard off of the high post is used in the Blast, UCLA, and Hawk offenses.

We suggest adding, changing, or modifying a form of the shell drill to include any other defensive situations that you feel suits your own coaching philosophy.

Practice Plans

This section offers a couple of different practice plans for your perusal. They are simply samples and they too can be modified as you see fit. Our practices are repetitive as we constantly strive to build a strong foundation for our team and organization. If we find there is slippage we place more emphasis on further developing a particular problem area to help improve our defense.

Pistons Training Camp Practice Plan

During training camp and throughout the 2003–2004 season we met every morning as a staff to discuss the day's practice, review video, and decide what we needed to work on and emphasize. Our goal was to get better each day. We discussed and viewed every game we played to help us understand the areas that needed improvement.

If we are in training camp and practicing twice a day we will meet before each practice. During the season, if the players have a day off or an optional practice, we still always meet as a staff to evaluate our performance and prepare for the next practice or game.

Morning Practice. A typical morning practice proceeds as follows:

1. Fast-break drill #1. Three lines full court. Passing back and forth for layups (passer, shooter, rebounder, outlet).
2. Progressive three. This is a three-man scripted weave: full court—five, four, and three passes for layups.
3. Four- and five-man scripted fast break with a trailing big man as a rebounder.
4. Full-court fast-break drill: Three against two, two against one, and one against one. On the two-against-one segment, the rebounder outlets to a coach stationed on either wing to begin the play, which makes the drill more realistic.
5. Shooting drill: Three players with two balls—three different individual offensive moves, in three one-and-a-half-minute segments; five groups of three with a water break once we rotate groups.
6. Shell defense drill: Half-court—four on four—introduce support position, guard-to-guard pass, guard-to-forward pass with cutter and baseline drive rotation. We then work on help and recover on a penetrating dribbler between two defenders.
7. Secondary script. Offense without defense—introduce Swing and Dive, two of our basic secondary offense plays.

8. Pick-and-roll drill from three spots from the UCLA set.

   ★ Wing or sideline pick and roll: Show/Under.
   ★ High pick and roll: Big defender plays centerfield and helps the dribbler's defender fight over the screen or go through.
   ★ Wing pick and roll: Trap and rotate.

9. Three-against-three full-court drill: Pass and screen away, dribble handoff, weave, pick and roll, pass and cut, jam screen defensive drill. We practice against each of these offensive options after first explaining how we want to defend them. The position of the ball in relation to your man is a point of emphasis that we constantly stress. See your man when you are on the strong side and be drawn to and see the ball when you are defending on the weak side.

10. Three-on-three half-court knockout drill: A team can only score while on defense. A team gets one point for a stop, but they also lose one point if they give up an offensive rebound. Zero points are awarded when a team fouls. We try to add one or two coaches on the perimeter as extra passers in this drill to make it more realistic.

11. Full-court defensive drill: Five-against-zero defense transition following a rebound or field goal. We go full court up and back scripting our full-court defense in relation to the position of the ball. We then add five offensive players and work on changing from offense to defense, matching up, and stopping the ball. We use this drill to script our trapping and pressing defenses.

12. Shooting drill: Three players with two balls; players who are not in groups on the court take a water break.

13. Set script #1: Wing entry pass setting up a wing or side pick and roll.

14. Post pass drill: Three-man turn out step-up game—backdoor with options—three players with each getting a shot on each possession.

15. Four-on-four keep-away drill: We count the number of passes a team makes without dribbles until they score a layup. We want to defend a segment of 24, 30, or 45 seconds. We also vary the drill to see how many passes are made before a team makes an open jump shot. This drill emphasizes all areas of defense as well as passing, ball and player movement, spacing, cutting, patience, taking care of the ball, and making the right decisions, both offensively and defensively.

16. End practice.

Players will work individually with coaches on shooting or ball-handling skills following each practice.

We also add a full-court defensive drill to our early practice schedule or practice outline. Our drills are designed to be as similar as possible to an actual game situation.

Evening or Late-Afternoon Practice

We will run the UCLA offensive set to set up three defensive pick-and-roll situations; we defend each pick-and-roll situation differently, as shown in Figure 5.41.

Following the point man's UCLA cut and clear out to the opposite corner we defend a wing pick and roll with a contact show on the screener and the dribbler's man quickly going under the screen as the screener's man gets back to his opponent by getting in the passing lane with his hands up. This is diagrammed in Figure 5.42.

Figure 5.41
UCLA cut and wing pick and roll where X⁵ contact shows and lets X² slide through to stop 2.

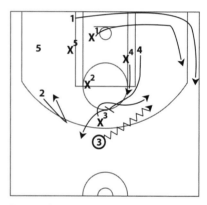

Figure 5.42
High pick and roll where X⁴ hard shows to stop the three-quarter HPR, letting X³ through as 4 fades or rolls to the basket.

Figure 5.43
Wing pick and roll: X¹ fights over the
screen and X⁵ tries to trap and stop
the ball with him.

Figure 5.44
X⁴ rotates to 5 and X⁵ doubles back to
4 unless X² has crossed the lane to
defend 4.

We then have the dribbler swing the ball to the top following a weak-side zipper exchange between the forward and wing where the forward who screened down then comes up to set a high screen and roll as the screener's defender helps the dribbler's man get through by showing hard to stop the ball. If 4 fades or pops back after his screen, X⁴ must recover to the screener. When 4 rolls to the goal we rotate big to big with X⁵ picking up the roll man. This action is shown in Figure 5.43.

Next, we then have the dribbler pass to the point guard who is now on the opposite wing and run another wing pick and roll, with the opposite big coming to set a screen from the weak-side low block. This time we trap the dribbler by having the big defender jumping out and turning the dribbler back to his defender. If 5 rolls or fades following his screen, we are ready to have X⁴ rotate to pick him up, as shown in Figure 5.44. X⁵ leaves the trap on the pass, rotating back to 4 or to the weak-side block if we have prerotated to 4 with X². When X⁴ pops we determine if we want him to recover to his man or if we want to prerotate again.

When we trap or double-team the ball the two defenders are called *trappers*. The next two defen-

Figure 5.45
Trap defense: X¹ and X⁵ seal the trap
(trappers). X³ and X⁴ are interceptors.
X² is the low goaltender. We are essen-
tially trapping in a 2-2-1 zone defense.

sive players nearest the ball act as *interceptors* and look to get in the passing lanes to steal or deflect the ball. The defender farthest from the ball guards the goal and the weak-side backboard. We call him the *high* or *low goaltender*, depending on the area where we are trapping the ball. We rotate our guards, wings, forwards, and centers to different positions and have them learn to defend each different situation on the court.

We feel it is a good idea each day to review and practice against an offensive set or play that you expect your team to see during the season.

The practice plans in this section are examples of organized practices, one from the NBA preseason and one from the end of a college season. We do not mean to imply that one practice plan is better or more efficient than the other.

When I coached overseas, we often played only once or twice a week unless we were in the playoffs when we played every other day. We normally had two practices every day. Our morning practice, which was between an hour and an hour and 15 minutes, was almost exclusively devoted to shooting and individual offensive skill development. At times, however, we also worked on our timing, spacing, and execution to keep things interesting. We also devoted an equal amount of time to our conditioning and weight training programs every other day. If players wanted to shoot during the days devoted to conditioning and weights, we would have a coach available to work with them on an individual or group basis. Our coaches in Detroit were always available to work with our players whenever they needed assistance or whenever the staff felt a player could benefit from some extra work. We always emphasized the importance of getting better each day.

Our late-afternoon practices overseas were usually from an hour and a half to a little more than two hours daily with defensive execution and game preparation as our major areas of emphasis. We also

Sample University of Portland Practice Plan #63—March 3, 2004

Offensive Emphasis of the Day:
Defensive Emphasis of the Day:
Thought for the Day:

Time	Minutes	Exercise
4:00–4:05	5	Discussion
4:05–4:15	10	Warm-up/Stretch
4:15–4:20	5	2 against 0 FB organization
4:20–4:27	7	3 against 2/2 against 1
4:27–4:35	8	3 against 2 Conditioner
4:35–4:40	5	Five-Man Transition— Scripting
4:40–4:50	10	3-Man/2-Ball Shooting Free Throws in Between
4:50–5:00	10	Post/Perimeter Stations Rebounding/Defense Guards—3 against 3, Fill and Sink Bigs—High-Low Flash, 2 against 2
5:00–5:20	20	Shell/Scout Interchanges, Box Screens
5:20–5:30	10	Secondary Live
5:30–5:40	10	Rebound Transition Game Offensive Rebound = 5 Points Defensive Rebound = 1 Point Break into Two Teams with Substitutes: White Black 1 2 3 4 5
5:40–5:50	10	Postpractice Comments

always scheduled day-of-game shootarounds and film sessions to review our game plan.

Practice with Defensive Stations

We determine the number of teaching stations by the number of coaches we have available as well as the number of half-courts and baskets. Stations can be varied or changed every day, but we want to teach our defensive tactics on a regular basis. We feel the use of stations is a very effective way to teach specific situations. It provides time for breaking down how we want to defend various offensive sets and game situations. In addition, it affords us time for individual instruction with our players. We might devote anywhere from 18 to 30 minutes for our station practice. We generally want to have at least two, and preferably three, teaching stations set up. We rotate our groups to another station every 6 to 10 minutes.

Example of Types of Stations

1. Pick-and-roll defense
2. Post defense
3. UCLA cut and pick and roll or down screen
4. Pin down and turn out
5. One-against-one defense (guarding the dribbler and keeping him in front of you a yard to either side)
6. Deny, help, and recover
7. One-against-one denial and close out
8. Defend the jam screen and flare
9. Defend cross screens
10. Isolations
11. Double-teaming from behind
12. Zigzag (one-against-one) drill pressuring and keeping an opponent in front of you in the full court
13. Keeping the offense out of the funnel or paint

Practices and Drills

We constantly create new practice plans and drills to build our team's skills and to keep things interesting. This section covers scrimmages and a three-against-two fast-break drill.

Scrimmages

1. We like to play up and down until one team scores. We defend against both a set offense and a transition team.
2. We start at one basket from either a half-court set or from out of bounds against a full court or half-court defense; go up and back down. We run a play at each end of the court for a total of three plays, rotate, and play until one of the teams has scored seven baskets.
3. We run plays from out of bounds and from different spots on the sideline and baseline. Teams have many opportunities to inbound from out of bounds during a game—following time-outs, substitutions, nonshooting fouls, turnovers, beginning of quarters or halves, and following made free throws. Your defense must be prepared to stop your opponents from scoring easy baskets in these situations.
4. We play a two-minute game and simulate end-of-game or end-of-quarter situations with one team ahead or behind in the score, and we stress getting stops by different defensive means.
5. We work on trying to steal the ball or fouling to stop the clock and lengthen the game if we are behind in the score.
6. We set up and run plays after a made or missed free throw and learn how to defend them.

7. We play five-on-zero offense on one end to five offensive players against five defensive players on the other end to five offensive players in transition after a steal, a rebound, or score against five defensive players in transition as they attack the basket on the other end of the court.

Three-Against-Two Fast-Break Drill

We find it beneficial to demonstrate how we want our defenders to play a tandem defense in this situation. First we break it down in a half-court setting to show the players their responsibilities before running the drill live on the full court.

When your team is outnumbered in the tandem defense the object is to protect the goal and force the offense to make an extra pass until transition defensive help arrives. We want to have the passer pick up his dribble and stop before he passes, enabling additional defensive help to arrive. In the conventional tandem defense the defender closest to the goal picks up the first pass to the wing as shown in Figure 5.46.

The point defender drops back to protect the basket, while also taking the next pass from the wing to the top or the skip pass over his head (Figures 5.47 and 5.48).

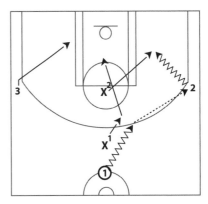

Figure 5.46
Three-against-two fast-break tandem defense: the taller defender is back and takes the first pass to wing (1 and 2).

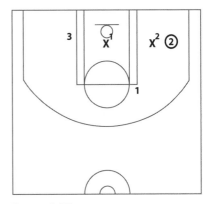

Figure 5.47
Ball is on the wing. X^2 plays ball and tries to contest and contain. X^1 retreats and covers goal and the weak-side backboard.

Figure 5.48
Pass from point to opposite wing.

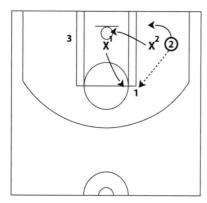

Figure 5.49
Pass back to point. X^1 plays ball. X^2 retreats and covers the goal. Some teams have X^2 cover 1 as X^1 covers the goal.

Some coaches instruct the bottom man of the tandem to then cover the second pass back to the top. In this case the back man would have the responsibility of covering the player receiving the cross-court skip pass (Figures 5.49 and 5.50).

We then go two against one on the return by having the offensive player who made the last shot (or whoever made the last pass) defend against the two tandem defenders, who now become the two offensive players attacking the opposite goal. This lone defender's responsibility is to protect the goal and stop the ball or force the offensive player with the ball to pick up his dribble until more defensive help arrives. We stress having the defender keep the ball and both offensive players in front of him to discourage layups.

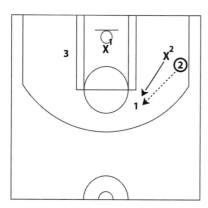

Figure 5.50
Defensive option: pass from wing back to point. X^2 follows pass. X^1 covers goal.

6

Defensive Principles
and Rebounding

Our defensive rules and the emphasis we place on rebounding we feel are the things that help us establish our defensive presence and mind-set.

Rules of Defense: Explanation of Different Defensive Weak-Side Help Alignments

We feel that weak-side defenders must always be in a position to provide help. They must be drawn to the ball to help shrink the floor. Our basic rule is that the help cannot get beat. For this to be true, our weak-side defenders must always provide help by moving on the pass and not on the catch. They must also occupy the nail and elbow and box defensive positions when not guarding the player with the ball. They are actually providing weak-side zone help.

Figure 6.1 shows the nail, elbow, and box defensive positions. In Figure 6.2 we see weak-side zone help.

Figure 6.3 illustrates the principle of getting the free man in the direction of the help when leaving the double-team or trap. This is normally dictated by where the pass out of the trap is made. The trapper is the runner once the pass is in the air.

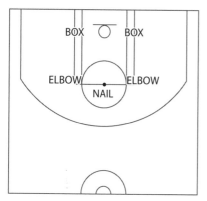

Figure 6.1
Nail, elbow, and box defensive positions.

Figure 6.2
Weak-side help: ball on wing (2); X^1 on strong-side elbow; X^2 on weak-side elbow; X^4 on weak-side box.

Defensive Principles We Require Our Players to Commit to Memory

When teams stress defense, we feel they tend to get more wins. Here is a list of the main defensive principles our players must constantly keep in mind.

1. Protect the paint. Stunt, shrink, sag, and dig when the basketball is below you or on the

post. Make low-post scoring opportunities difficult. Get level with the ball when not guarding the player with the ball.

2. Keep the lane compact to stop penetration and the straight-line drive. Make teams try to beat you from outside and force them to shoot over you with your hand up.

3. Randomly double-team the post by snapping back off of cutters once the cutter has reached the goal.

4. When defending pick and rolls we sometimes change our coverage and use an aggressive show or soft double-team until the ball is stopped. If we play up on the dribbler, it is difficult to get screened.

5. Rotate out of traps according to the flight of the ball. If the ball is swung to the weak side over the trapper's head, he should try to recover to his man. If the ball is thrown back to the screener on the strong side, the closest big man will rotate to the screener and the original defender will rotate to the free man in the direction of the help.

6. When defending against the pick and roll, the screener's man must contact show by keeping in contact with the screener as he jumps out to stop the dribbler before quickly getting back into the passing lane with his hands up as he recovers to the screener as he rolls to the goal.

7. When the defender plays aggressive pick-and-roll defense on the screener, he leaves himself open to quick slips. Therefore, it is imperative that the weak-side defenders are in position on the elbows and boxes to rotate quickly to pick up the slip man.

8. The off-the-ball defenders need to be aware of and be drawn to the ball at all times if they are to rotate and provide weak-side help.

Figure 6.3
Trapping the low post from the post feeder (X^2) on pass from 5 to 1. X^1 takes 1, X^3 rotates to X^3 from the weak-side elbow, and X^2 rotates out of the trap and takes X^4 as the ball is swung from 1 to 3 to 2.

9. We will sometimes force the pick and roll down the sideline to deny the offense the opportunity to reverse and change sides with the ball. This is an especially effective tactic when the ball-side corner is filled, but it can also be used in many other circumstances.

10. We will at times push up and squeeze or hug any screener on or off the ball. We will push or body the screener into his offensive teammate to help the defender quickly get under the screen and back to his opponent. We can also have the screener's defender step back to let his defensive teammate through.

11. We spend time teaching our big men to anticipate the pick and roll and jump before the screen can be set by having a signal that alerts our weak-side defenders to this tactic.

12. We want to get back in transition quickly to set up our defense and limit easy basket opportunities.

13. We need at least two and a half offensive rebounders and have to guard against leak-outs on our jump shooters or penetrators.

14. We continually emphasize ball pressure, getting into the passing lanes, and full body show to stop penetration.

15. We want to extend our defense to the back-court and force the opposition to bring the ball up versus pressure to force them to make as many decisions as possible before they can settle into an offensive rhythm.

16. We always try to close out on shooters under control and with a hand up.

17. It is important to keep your individual opponent in front of you. This becomes even more important if your team doesn't have a shot blocker defending the middle to intimidate shooters and reject shots.

18. Defense is about effort and determination more than athletic ability. You must estab-

lish accountability on defense. Do not tolerate slippage.

19. You must establish consistency in the way you defend. Defense is every night. Defense cannot have bad days.

20. We want our players to understand that we may change our defense during a time-out or when our opponent is taking the ball out of bounds. The type of defense you play can be determined by the time on the shot clock and/or the area of the court where the ball will be put in play. For example, you might want to play some kind of normal zone, a three–two match-up, a shadow or tilt defense, a trapping defense after dead-ball situations, or anything you have practiced that you feel will confuse or disrupt the opposition.

21. We try to give our opponents multiple looks when we defend the pick and roll, but we normally begin with our standard coverage.

22. We want to know where our opponent intends to go with the ball. Then we can anticipate and influence where we want the ball to go and whether we want to force the ball middle or sideline. We will probably force middle if we have a shot blocker behind us.

23. Our defense is predicated on not permitting ball reversal. We emphasize this during every practice and game.

24. We try to stretch out, deny, and pressure penetrating passes. We want our opponents to catch or receive the ball out of the scoring areas and as far out on the perimeter as possible.

25. We explain and teach the proper defensive stance to our players. We want the knees bent and the player in a boxer's stance when guarding a player facing the basket with the dribble live. We want the defender to take a

Big Ben Wallace of the 2003–2004 NBA Champion Detroit Pistons comes to play defense every night, and nobody protects the paint like he does. Here he is pictured rejecting the shot of Shareef Abdur-Raheem, then of the Atlanta Hawks.
Photo courtesy of NBA Entertainment.

We constantly stress to our players the importance of contesting every shot. In this photo NBA veteran Derrick Coleman of the Philadelphia 76ers, goes up to challenge the shot of the massive Yao Ming of the Houston Rockets.
Photo courtesy of NBA Entertainment.

direct fake on his back foot. He can then recover or step back and pivot to force and angle the offensive player away from the basket while keeping the dribbler in front of him.

26. One method we use to motivate our players defensively is using the clock and keeping score during practices.

27. We play a great deal of full-court three against three, four against four, and five against five in our practices, which tends to keep things competitive.

28. When defending a post feeder we prefer the feeder's defender to get level with the ball with his back to the baseline enabling him to force the cutter to go one way instead of giving him a choice. We are able to efficiently help and dig on the post from this position.

29. If we don't permit offensive rebounds (in other words, if we limit second-shot opportunities), stop fast-break baskets, take care of the basketball, and keep our opponents off the free-throw line, we will win most games.

30. At the end of a close game it is not the shot that beats you—it's the offensive rebound. Your players cannot stand around hoping the last shot doesn't go in the basket. Instead they must box out, rebound, and secure the ball.

Defensive Points Your Players Should Commit to Memory

Although all of the principles listed above are important and usable, the following six points will be the most important as you begin to build your team's defensive skills.

1. Always be ready to help and rotate to the ball from the weak side.
2. Pressure the basketball.
3. The player guarding the screener must hedge, stay connected, and show on all on ball screens.
4. Switch everything in short-clock situations. Take something away from the offense. Force them uphill and away from the basket. Limit them to one bad shot.
5. Help and recover on strong-side shooters.
6. Maintain good floor balance as an aid to great transition defense.

Defending the Low Post

Do you want to play behind, front, or three-quarter the low post? We think you must be consistent and demand that your players understand that you always want to defend the post based on the position of the ball. Your decision should depend in part on where you want your help defense to come from. You can always adjust how you play a particular scheme after your team has mastered and understood the basic general tactic.

Most of the focus should be on stopping, disrupting, and taking something away from your opponent. How you accomplish this is determined by your philosophy. Your primary focus should be on teaching and preparing your own team. You should want your opponents to adjust and match up to you. For instance, find out how many opponents play zones so you can decide how much time you should devote to practicing against opposition zones and to practicing your own zones.

Drill on how to front the post and how to defend the flash post on ball reversal. Teammates must develop trust in each other. Post defenders will be more apt to front the post if they know their teammates will pressure the passer and that the weak-side

Defending the low post can be a challenge for defenders. Here, Chauncey Billups of the Detroit Pistons attempts to guard the much larger Aaron McKie of the Philadelphia 76ers.
Photo courtesy of NBA Entertainment.

defenders will be watching their backs, shrinking the floor, and rotating to help.

You must take away position when defending an opponent's offense. Don't allow them to set up where they want and don't permit them to make uncontested entry passes. The defender guarding the passers and the defender whose man wants to receive the ball have equal responsibility when it comes to forcing the receiver to grab the ball in a less than advantageous position.

When fronting the post we want to be in a position to trap and/or double the baseline drive and to rotate to protect the goal by having our weak-side defenders drawn to the basketball.

When digging on the post or helping to stop penetration it is very important to give full-body help to force the pass to be made over the help defender's outside shoulder—or to get in the way of the player who has the ball and pick up an offensive foul.

When teaching post defense it is useful to divide the half-court into quarters. This will enable you to demonstrate to your players how to defend the post by having them understand that the location of the ball and the position of the player on the post dictate whether they should front, three-quarter, or lock in and play one half a man to prevent the spin lob.

We feel it's important to emphasize to your players that fronting the post requires effort as well as determination. Aggressively fighting for position is a requirement for an outstanding low-post defender.

It is difficult to front the post effectively when the basketball is at the top of the key or circle because it is very tough to get weak-side help. With the ball in this position it is much better to play half a man and body up to the offensive post player to prevent the spin lob. When the basketball moves around the perimeter you can then decide to front or three-quarter the offensive player. Teach your players to step up and over the front foot of the offensive player as the ball is passed around the perimeter. If we play behind the post man we want our players to use their legs and the palm of one hand to try and route the offensive player off the post, as far from the basket as possible. When we do front we want to sit on the offensive player's legs denying him a good comfortable position as well as the ability to jump to receive a lob pass. Post defenders must be schooled in using their hands to deflect post entry passes and in using active hands to deflect or steal the ball when the post player dribbles with his back to the basket. The post defenders must constantly use tactics that disrupt the offensive post player's rhythm. Our objective is to force the post players out of their comfort zone.

We work diligently on fronting the low post because it is a primary defensive weapon in our arsenal. Many teams respond to the defense fronting the post by flashing a man to the high post in order to execute the high-low pass in the paint. If we push the post man off the block when we cannot front him and he does receive the basketball but cannot score and passes the ball out in order to improve his position on the low post, our rule is that the post defender must again work to front his opponent. We front the post to keep the ball out of the middle and to be in position to trap the baseline drive.

Rebounding

You must limit your opponents to one shot. Permitting them to grab offensive rebounds really jeopardizes your defense. Your players must be aware of the opponent's potential to tap out loose rebounds they cannot control. This situation represents yet another reason why you must rebound with all *five* defenders. You cannot permit second shots and putbacks if you want to be successful. Many teams rely heavily on gang-style offensive rebounding, a tactic that will put increased pressure on your defense. We constantly stress the importance of not allowing the opponent second-shot opportunities because baskets scored after a team rebounds a missed shot are the shots that will get our team beat. Your team must always anticipate the miss, and rebounders must follow the flight of the ball. Take no chances. Grab the rebound or loose ball with both hands to control it.

Individual Defense, Team Defense, and Drills

7

This chapter will take a look at individual and team defense and drills you can use to help improve your team in both areas.

Individual Defense

The foundation of great defense is made up of footwork, balance, determination, conditioning, and practice. Constant repetition will help your players learn how to defend. Remember that it is much easier for a player to retain what you teach when you explain the situations in which he will use a particular skill. For example, simply showing him how to take a direct fake on his back foot may not be sufficient. If you explain *why* you are asking him to do this and then show him how, by staying low, he can pivot and control his man and how this will also help him close out, he will be much more apt to master the technique.

When discussing how we want to play a man with the ball on the wing we use the following set of rules we practice to stop penetration and avoid a straight-line drive to the basket:

1. Force the offensive player toward the sideline by having your knees bent and your outside foot forward and outside his outside shoulder to influence him in that direction. Your goal is to keep your opponent one yard in front of you on either side.
2. Take a direct fake by dropping your back foot.
3. Keep your hands spread with the palms up to apply pressure, hinder passes, and cause deflections.
4. By forcing sideline your goal is to angle the opponent and cut off his drive at the baseline hash mark.
5. Should the offensive player try to drive middle, force him uphill toward the center of the court and away from the basket.

6. When denying the penetrating pass on the wing never get above the ball where the offensive player can easily freeze you and go backdoor. Stay even and force him to catch the ball farther out on the perimeter unless your team is in all-out steal-the-ball defensive mode.

7. Stay down and maintain a low center of gravity when the opponent drives. You cannot stop him if you stand up or bob up and down.

Individual Defense: Important Things a Defender Must Remember

1. Don't permit dribble penetration. Pressure the basketball and keep it in front of you.
2. Try to create turnovers and draw offensive fouls.
3. Always be drawn to the ball when defending offensive players away from the ball. Don't turn your head.
4. Anticipate the miss. Rebound every shot.
5. Always box out on defense and follow the flight of the ball when rebounding. Don't jump until you know where the ball is going
6. The passer makes the play. Always watch and be aware of his cuts.
7. Continually be ready to guard the passer, cutter, and players moving without the ball.
8. Don't let the offense pass the ball inside, out, and over when your team is playing zone defense. Stop ball reversal and be aware of teams attacking the zone from behind. Play defense with your hands up to discourage easy passes.
9. Try to familiarize yourself with your opponent's plays, tendencies, calls, and signals.

10. Don't let the offense establish passing lanes against the zone. Don't permit them to improve position to gain possession.

11. Be prepared to rotate back to cover the goal when playing weak-side defense. Be drawn toward the ball.

12. Don't permit the offense to beat your zone down court. Attack your opponent before they can set up offensively and get established.

13. Normal out-of-bounds plays may be less effective against zones since teams sometimes neglect to practice against zones on out-of-bounds situations.

14. Definitely try to make the simple play rather than the spectacular one.

15. Don't commit foolish fouls. Always be aware of time, score, and situation.

16. Don't commit a personal foul that could result in a three-point play.

17. Grab all loose balls and rebounds with two hands. Control of the ball is essential.

18. Strive not to foul a team that shoots a high free-throw percentage.

19. Don't let your opponents put you in jeopardy. Keep them off the free-throw line.

20. Use your hands to try to deflect passes and limit opponents' passing lanes when defending.

21. Contest every perimeter shot the opposition takes—but do it *without* committing a foul.

22. Remember, when the ball is in the middle of the floor there is no strong side. Try to pressure up and force your opponent to receive the ball higher up on the perimeter.

23. When providing help to stop penetration or to steal the ball, don't run directly at the dribbler or shooter; instead run to a spot just in front of him. You must beat your opponent to the spot.

24. Remember, the help cannot get beat. Players helping off the ball must stop dribble penetration.

Rules of Individual Defense

1. Always pressure the ball.
2. Deny or overplay the next penetrating pass.
3. Don't permit easy ball reversal. Keep the ball on one side of the court.
4. Move on the pass, not on the catch.
5. Box out your individual opponent when rebounding defensively and fast break and run off of defensive rebounds.
6. See the ball and your man. Adhere to the ball-you-man principle (keep your body between your man and the ball).
7. Bump, chuck, and/or bodycheck all cutters.
8. Defend with your body and by moving your feet.
9. Make yourself as long and wide as possible.
10. Open to the ball and retreat to the basket when your man goes backdoor, or snap back and take your opponent into the lane to deny him the ball.
11. Help and recover to stop dribble penetration. Provide full body help.
12. The shooter is the most dangerous rebounder. Box him out.
13. Always help from the weak side. You should always be drawn to the ball to shrink the floor.
14. Sprint back and rotate to the free man in the direction of the help.
15. Always try to be level with the ball.
16. Multiply and immediately apply pressure after scoring an easy layup.
17. Learn to slip the pick. Don't permit yourself to be screened.

Playing individual defense can be a great challenge to younger players. Here, the 19-year-old Serbian-born Darko Milicic gets ready to defend the speedy Tim Thomas, then of the Milwaukee Bucks. Photo courtesy of NBA Entertainment.

18. Jump out and aggressively switch when equal-size players screen for one another with or without the ball. Turn the offensive player with the ball back to his defender. Always take something away from your opponent. Seal and don't permit the offense to split the switch, trap, or double-team. The help cannot be beat.

19. Always talk and communicate with your teammates when playing defense.

20. In short-clock situations, aggressively step out and switch regardless of size differences. Don't let the offense split the switch. Defenders must come together and seal the man with the ball.

21. Don't chase the back-picker. Beware of screening your own teammate.

22. Pressure and close out on all shooters. Contest all shots and stop dribble penetration.

23. Maintain defensive balance at all times to stop early transition baskets.

24. Always see the ball and retreat to the goal and make yourself bigger if you lose sight of your man. The ball will always take you to your man. Work to backpedal and get level with the ball.

25. Always change quickly from offense to defense and sprint back in defensive transition.

26. Don't permit the offensive player to get to your body and seal or hold you off.

27. Talk, Talk, Talk. Help your teammates.

28. When trapping or double-teaming the player with the ball, make the offensive player find the free man farthest from the ball to give the defense the time and opportunity to rotate effectively.

29. Force offensive players using screens to go only one way. Don't allow them a choice or option.

30. Play all high-post players as if they had used their dribble. Pressure the ball so they cannot easily feed the post or reverse the ball and move the defense.

One-on-One Defensive Drill from the Wing

Our players must work on keeping their man in front of them and forcing the offensive player with the ball toward the sideline to the baseline hash mark or to a predetermined spot on the baseline. We want to keep the man with the ball from penetrating to the goal. If he attempts to drive the middle, we want to force him away from the goal and as far out of the paint as possible by using the corners as our guideline (Figure 7.1).

Individual Defense Checklist

1. Use proper stance and footwork. Keep your weight low to enable you to move quickly laterally, forward, or backward.
2. Use your hands effectively. There's more to it than just "Hands up!" Keep one hand planted in the ball handler's gut to prevent him from bringing the ball up into shooting position.
3. Use floor position to your advantage. Each player's defensive position will depend on the defensive scheme your team is playing, e.g., zone or man-to-man, deny trap, help, or hedge. Shrink the floor.
4. Guard the back-to-the-basket player in the paint or low post; front the pivot player.
5. Rebound. Block out, time the carom, follow the flight of the ball, and don't jump until you see where the ball is going.
6. Boxer analogy: If you are in the proper stance, balanced, and moving your feet

How do you stop the NBA's most unstoppable force? Here, two-time NBA MVP Tim Duncan of the San Antonio Spurs refuses to allow Shaquille O'Neal an easy basket. Photo courtesy of NBA Entertainment.

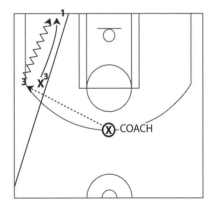

Figure 7.1
One on one from the wing: defender X³ forces 3 to a spot on the baseline, but outside the lane. Defender must also deny the middle.

effectively, you should be able to throw a knockout punch at your opponent.

7. Linebacker analogy: When defending a penetrating dribbler, you should be in a position to tackle him head-on if you have moved your feet effectively to prevent a straight-line drive to the basket.

8. When defending a player without the ball *always* see the ball and your man.

9. Use proper movements and alignment in defending against the fast break (e.g., three against two; two against one).

Note: This checklist is a bare-bones outline that requires demonstration and then repetition of the skills. No matter what defensive schemes are used, the basic fundamentals—stance, footwork, and use of hands—are essential. There are a host of individual defensive drills that can be employed in teaching individual defense fundamentals. Your players must learn to run, move, change direction, backpedal, and pivot quickly while running laterally or sideways if they want to be good defenders. The key is to maintain a low center of gravity until you are close to the basket and have to defend a shot. Then you must stand straighter and make yourself bigger. The ability to run backward at high speed is a unique skill and one that must be practiced.

Every team looks for defensive stoppers. It is the coach's responsibility to find out which of his players relishes this role. Once you determine your best defensive players, you must find a way to put them on the floor since they will help your team win. Successful coaches put their players in situations where they can succeed.

A team's defensive stoppers used to be called gloves, but these days we call a glove a blanket. When we want to deny and stop a player we tell our defender to "marry" his opponent and only look to help out when he and his opponent are on the weak side away from the basketball.

We use the one-against-one zigzag drill to teach our players how to keep opponents in front of them and to get them used to forcing the dribbler to change direction and make quick decisions. If the defender is beaten off the dribble, we teach him to release and run to a spot to again get in front of his opponent so he can keep him in front of him.

Defense begins with ball pressure. Roy Williams, the former coach at Kansas who is now at North Carolina, teaches his defensive players to keep their individual opponents a yard in front of them on either side to stop penetration. Without good individual defense there can be no trust. Keep your opponent in front of you. Stop dribble penetration and eliminate the straight-line drive to the basket. Always try to force the dribbler to stop and pick up the basketball. If your players try to guard, they will get better and earn the right to play.

When controlling your man a yard to either side, you cannot turn and play on the side of your man. Guard against giving your opponent a clear path to the basket. Your feet should actually be set at a right angle to help you influence the offensive player toward the side where you want him to dribble.

It is easier to take a direct fake on your back foot if your feet are at a right angle rather than parallel because you don't have to first drop a foot and pivot before retreating.

I asked Pete Carril, the legendary former Princeton University coach who is now an assistant coach of the Sacramento Kings, to give me his favorite defensive drill for this book and he explained a one-on-one drill that he's always used with his players. It's a three-man drill using a passer, a defender, and an offensive player. They are all on the half-court, placed wherever the coach wants them (see Figure 7.2). The defender must stop the offensive player; once this is accomplished he switches to offense, the offensive player becomes the passer, and the passer becomes the new defensive player. This differs from the usual offense-to-defense-to-passer rotation.

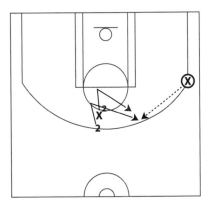

Figure 7.2
Pete Carril's one-against-one game of seven stops: Begin from different spots on the half-court. If X^2 stops 2 from scoring, X^2 becomes offensive player, passer becomes the defender, and offensive player becomes the passer.

Points are given only for defensive stops and can be played to five or seven stops before the game is over. This drill teaches discipline and rewards the players only when they get stops (Figure 7.2).

Team Defense

All defense should be built on a solid foundation of basic fundamentals that are consistent with your philosophy.

A team might play a number of different half-court defenses depending on the game's time (game and shot clock), score, and situation. They might give each defense a name, color, number, key word, or signal. The decision to change defenses or which one to play at any given time will most likely be explained during a time-out, but teams should be prepared to change during a dead-ball situation as well. Here's an example:

1. Normal half-court man-to-man defense.

   ★ Overplay and deny all penetrating passes one pass away from the ball.
   ★ Pressure the ball and play all big men on the perimeter as though the dribble was used.
   ★ Stay level with the ball and don't overplay the pass back to the top.
   ★ Front the low post.
   ★ Play weak-side defense by making sure the nail, elbows, and low blocks or boxes are always occupied.

2. Half-court pressure man-to-man defense to change the game's tempo.

   ★ Deny all passes to players one pass away from the ball and play all high post players as though the dribble was used.
   ★ Apply aggressive on-the-ball pressure at all times.

★ Force your opponent to put the ball on the floor, but keep him in front of you and limit his ability to penetrate.

★ All our help will come from the second man removed unless the dribbler has his back turned or our trapper is two or three strides away from the ball and we are able to run and jump and/or surprise and trap the dribbler.

3. Short-clock or crunch-time defense.

★ In out-of-bounds situations, invert and switch all crosses, screens, and ball exchanges.

★ Switch aggressively on all crosses, screens, and ball exchanges

Summary of Team Defense Emphasis

Teach your team how to defend each of the following situations:

Quick post-ups and post-ups from
    offensive sets
Weak-side curls, turnouts, dives, and flex cuts
Post cuts and splits—baseline, middle, and
    weak-side areas
Jam screens, flares, fades, and slips
Draw and kick moves (penetrate and pitch)
Dribble hand-offs
On-the-ball screens
Cross screens (big-on-big, small-on-big, etc.)
Utah up blocks
Hawk cuts
UCLA cuts
Staggered screens
Up-the-line screens
Pick the picker screens
Isolations
Zipper screens
Step-ups and step-up flare action
Screen and pop-backs
Diagonal screens

Loops: cuts over and under screeners
Wide curls, backdoor cuts, back picks,
   down screens, and turnouts

You must especially emphasize the following:

Defensive rotation rules—how weak-side
   defenders provide help in order to
   rotate properly
Plug (nail), elbow, and box weak-side
   principles
Weak-side help (support)
The principle that the ball will always take
   you to your man
Getting level with the ball when defending
   off the ball

Defensive Coverages: "The Dirty 30"

The follow list, which I came across in some notes,
is another example of a coach categorizing and developing a list of things he wants his team to learn to
defend.

1. Motion
2. Side pick and roll
3. High pick and roll
4. Small/small pick and roll
5. Step up pick and roll
6. Cross action/pick and roll
7. Cross action pin down
8. UCLA action
9. UCLA pick and roll
10. Hawk action
11. Hawk action pick and roll
12. Dribble handoff
13. Dig and dive
14. Splits
15. Rubs/slash
16. Drop
17. "V" actions
18. Sideline out of bounds plays
19. Baseline out of bounds plays

20. Free-throw block-outs
21. Live cutters
22. Transition defense
23. Stance/post and perimeter
24. Flares
25. Rip screens: back picks
26. Seven-in-one drill: individual defensive drill in relation to the ball
27. Post-ups
28. Slips by screeners
29. Blitz pin downs
30. Misdirection screens

In case there is any doubt left in your mind, different coaches have very different ways of emphasizing the same things, and many use their own particular terminology.

Philosophy of Team Defense

When it comes to good team defense, aggressive on-the-ball pressure is important and can never be neglected. It sets the tone and your team's mind-set. You must disrupt your opponent's rhythm and not let them get into a smooth offensive flow. The more you can make your opponents change direction with the dribble and/or turn their backs, the more successful you will be. Force the dribbler to dribble at top speed with his head down. If he beats you, release and get to a spot in front of him. Make him uncomfortable. Your defensive goal should always be to take something away from your opponent. Be the aggressor. Your ultimate goal should be to limit penetration and force hurried or bad shots with a hand up in a shooter's face. Don't permit layups or straight-line drives to the basket. Force your opponent to make a pressured and hurried extra pass.

I once read a newspaper article quoting Hubie Brown, coach of the NBA's Memphis Grizzlies. He said his team has a goal of having at least seven defensive deflections in each quarter. This statistic helps them to measure their defensive pressure and

Figure 7.3
Slipping the screen: as 4 tries to screen X², X² moves toward the ball and does not permit 4 to screen him as X⁴ steps back and lets him through. (The ball is across the court and not on the strong side.)

Figure 7.4
Screening the defender: 4 screens X⁴. X² reads this and comes inside the screen and causes 2 to fade. (The ball is across the court and not on the strong side.)

aggressiveness. One of his assistant coaches charts deflections during the game and constantly reminds the players of whether or not they are accomplishing their goal.

Defending Single Screens

One of the primary things players must remember in defending against a player who wants to use a screen is never to let the offensive player get to their body. The offensive opponent will try to set you up and freeze you to get free before coming off of the screen. You must move and not permit them to close the distance between the two of you when they try to get free. Defenders must learn to slip screens and avoid being picked off (Figure 7.3). Teams often have their offensive players screen their own defenders to combat switching defenses and this helps to set up mismatches (Figure 7.4). We encourage our players to try to force the player using the screen away from the screener. *The idea is for our defender to force his opponent one way and not allow him a choice.* We want a player who traps to turn the player with the ball back to his defender. We also employ this tactic when we jump-switch a dribbler (Figure 7.5). We want our defender to move and slip the pick to deny

Figure 7.5
Trapping the dribbler on the elbow pick and roll: X⁴ traps 1 and sends him back uphill to X¹.

the screener a shot at his body (see Figure 7.3). A moving defender is a difficult target to screen and may cause your opponents to commit an offensive foul.

We always want to read the offense. If we can stand-up the screener and not let him screen where he wants to, we are helping a teammate who is defending against the screen. Whether we trail or go through or over when defending the down screen or the screen away usually depends on the position of the ball. If it is in the middle of the court and no weak side or strong side has been declared, we usually prefer to lock and trail and get to the outside shoulder and hip of the man receiving the screen (Figure 7.9). If the basketball is on the weak side, however, we prefer to have the screener's defender step back to provide his teammate with a path to get through and beat the offensive player to the spot he wants. We sometimes allow him to slide through in front of the screener and his defender to make the offensive player fade to the corner (Figure 7.7). Many times we also play on the top and outside of the offensive player to force him baseline and to the other side of the floor (Figure 7.6). Pressure on the passer also helps the player guarding the screener. We are always prepared to vary our coverage should the offense be gaining an advantage. If the offense screens their own defenders we will try to shoot the gap and come inside and beat the man receiving the screen to the spot rather than locking and trailing since there is no help from the screener's defender. We will also try to make the offensive player fade once he reaches the screen.

We will often switch up the line when defending against multiple screens. We will also go over the first screen and under the second screen. Again we encourage the men defending the screeners to stay connected and stand up the screeners to make the offense catch the ball farther out on the floor. In certain situations we may also lock and trail and jump-switch and trap the receiver as soon as he catches the ball (Figure 7.8).

Figure 7.6
Playing topside and forcing the player one way: X¹ must pressure the ball.

Figure 7.7
4 screens down on X⁴, and X³ comes inside and forces 3 to fade to the corner. X¹ must pressure the pass.

Figure 7.8
Switching up the line: 4 and 5 set a staggered double screen for 2 as X⁵ jumps out and switches to get in the passing lane to turn 2 back.

Figure 7.9
Lock and trailing and jump switching and trapping on the pass: it is important that X⁴ traps 2 and turns him back and that X² and X⁵ trap 2.

We do not want to chase the back picker when defending a player setting a back pick. We never want to screen our own teammate by playing too close to the screener (Figure 7.10).

Defending Cross Screens

You may want to vary your tactic when defending screens set by players of equal size or when a smaller player sets a screen for a bigger player. Some teams switch all the time, regardless of size differences, and many teams switch everything in short- or late-clock situations. A player must decide whether to body up and force the cutter over the screen, ride him low, or go under the screen and beat him to the spot while a teammate guarding the screener bumps and holds up the offensive man until you can go under and reach a spot in front of the offensive player (Figures 7.11 and 7.12).

These are decisions you as a coach have to make. You must be consistent. We believe in teaching and mastering one defensive tactic first. It is our feeling that we can always make adjustments if an opponent is giving us trouble. Our goal is to first build a solid

Figure 7.10
Defending back picks: 2 back screens X⁴ as 4 dives to the post. X² cannot chase 2 because if he does, he will screen his teammate and give up a lob or a dunk.

defensive foundation before we begin to vary our coverages.

We continue to work on defense all season long. We try to break down all our drills into two-against-two, three-against-three, or four-against-four situations in order to practice our defensive tactics.

We set up three or four teaching stations in our practices and rotate players to stations where we have coaches assigned to drill each situation. We get a great deal accomplished via this system, and we are able to give greater emphasis and individual attention to each area and to each of our players as well. We put both big men and perimeter players together at our stations to make our players comfortable executing with each other in realistic game situations.

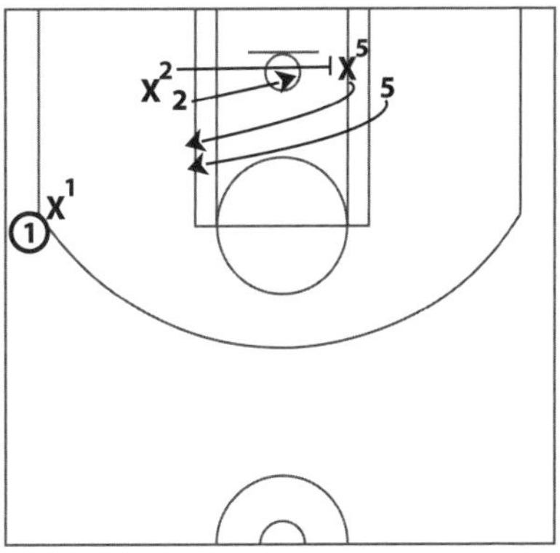

Figure 7.11
Defending cross screens; bodying up; forcing player over the screen.

Trapping the Low Post

Decide how and when you want to defend the post and if and when you want to dig, trap, or double-team post players or outstanding individual players. Will you continually trap the post on every possession, or will you utilize the one-and-done principle, trapping once and then falling back into your standard defense? We spend a great deal of time practicing helping and digging against post players with the basketball. This helps our interceptors know when to go for steals and when to stay at home.

Our goal in trapping the low post is twofold. First, we want to keep the low-post player from dominating inside; second, we want to disrupt the offense by taking something away from them to create steal opportunities for our perimeter defenders. We try to initiate our traps in the following situations:

Figure 7.12
X^2 bumps or slows 5 as X^5 goes under screen by X^2 and beats 5 to his post-up position to front.

1. When a specific player receives the ball in his prime or most effective area on the low block
2. When the post player puts the ball on the floor (one or two dribbles)

3. When the offensive player with the ball turns his back toward the baseline away from the nearest perimeter defender
4. Once we recognize the opportunity for an isolation play
5. When the post feeder cuts and once the defender's opponent has taken him to the goal, he can double back and trap the post player

Our normal or basic defensive strategy is to always front the low post. Our primary goal is to prevent the ball from being passed inside, enabling us to stay home on perimeter shooters. Most offenses like to go inside, out, and over. We want to discourage this tactic and keep the ball from being reversed. We must always be prepared to trap a post player on the low block once the ball is caught inside. Our perimeter players must learn how to dig, rotate, and recover or bump back to the shooters on the perimeter.

When we trap we want to turn the man we trap to the outside and back to his defender to take away his move to the middle. The trapper must also come with his arms extended to pressure a pass or shot and lock his inside leg with his teammate's to deny the penetrating or gut pass. We don't want to foul or bail out the offensive player by reaching for the ball.

We trap the low post from many different areas depending on the strengths and weaknesses of the opposition. We vary when and where our trappers come from, making it more difficult for our opponents to prepare for us. We may trap with the feeder's defender, off of the opposition's worst shooter, from the top of the key, with the nearest big man, or from the weak-side baseline. Our traps are designed to disrupt and cause our opponents to be indecisive.

We designate the areas of the court where we prefer to initiate our half-court traps. We trap in the mid-court areas where the sideline and mid-court line intersect and in the corners where the sideline and baseline meet. In these areas the lines are your allies and you can trap a player on all four sides.

Strategy and Tactics

How do you want to defend the penetrating pass? Do you want to deny and overplay? Do you want to make the offensive player receive the ball higher up on the perimeter? Will you emphasize the ball-you-man principle in a one-pass-away situation?

How will you play weak-side defense? What about transition defense? Do you emphasize leveling with the ball, staying with your individual opponent, or quickly changing ends and getting back to a particular position? Do you double the baseline drive when you front the post? How do you play cross screens, pick and rolls, curls, flares, turnouts, fades, jam screens, and staggered screens?

How do you teach your players to stop penetration (shell drill)? You must decide if you want to force the ball sideline or if you want to channel everything to the middle of the floor. Where do you want to begin your defense? How much pressure do you want to exert? These are decisions you have to make, plan, and teach to prepare your players to meet every challenge. No matter which tactics you choose, your team must accept the fact that defense is *vital*.

Former NBA great Jerry West, president of the NBA's Memphis Grizzlies, spoke at a coaching meeting where he said, "Better defensive players turn games around. Players who are able to take shots away from shooters are rare, and players who can come up with loose balls are an even greater rarity." We believe players with these attributes will definitely help you win.

Practice Drills and Objectives

We believe in teaching fundamentals all season long, not exclusively during preseason preparation. We break some of our practice time down into separate big- and small-man drills, as well as drills mixing and using both perimeter and post players.

We want competitive defensive drills that emphasize game situations and stimulate the will to win. Many of our defensive drills force the defenders to get stops before they can rotate to offense. At times we reward teams getting stops by rotating offensive teams if they don't score, only awarding points for stops while keeping the defenders on the floor. We have found that this helps to eliminate boredom during practices. Players love to compete, and anything that can get the competitive juices going will capture their attention and keep them interested. The higher you set the bar, the better the results. Players have no real limitations if you work with them. Any coach who can improve a player's game will gain that player's respect. Many times we have the first team scrimmage our second team, and it is usually a war, but on occasion we mix both groups together. This creates an entirely different set of circumstances. It also gives us an idea of which players play well together and complement each other.

Shell Defensive Drill

We like to use the shell drill throughout the season— almost every day if possible. Our shell drill is normally a four-against-four half-court defensive drill that can be played three against three as well. It can also be extended to the full or three-quarter court. We begin by demonstrating to our players the stance and position we prefer them to be in when guarding a man with the ball, and the proper stance and positioning when defending players one or two passes away in help or support positions. To accomplish this, we place the ball in each of four positions on the floor and show the players off of the ball how we want them to be positioned. We explain and show them how we want them to defend and overplay and how to deny the penetrating pass. We then demonstrate why and how we want them to jump in the direction of the ball when it is passed, *not* when it is caught, how the ball should draw them to it when guarding the passer or any player who does not have the ball.

A great deal of our teaching emphasis is based on the players understanding their relationship to the position of the ball on the court as well as whether the initial pass is a guard-to-guard pass or a guard-to-forward pass. The next step is teaching how we prefer to guard cutters or players screening away and how we defend down screens or back picks. This is a step-by-step process, one that requires constant drill and repetition. We also set up draw-and-kick and help-and-recover situations to help the team learn how to stop dribble penetration and close out on shooters to contest shots. We also incorporate defending on-the-ball screens in this drill. The shell drill is played without an offensive low- or high-post man because we want to encourage quick reaction in a wider defensive area while continuing to emphasize the importance of weak-side help. We explain and reinforce this by having our low-post defenders front the low post and learn to play man-to-man, one-against-one post defense.

We demonstrate positioning with an offensive high- or low-post player by setting up an offensive alignment on the court to show our players how we want to defend a particular set in relation to the ball. We do this before we practice against any offensive set. We feel that this teaching technique eliminates confusion and provides an opportunity for our players to ask questions when they do not understand why we defend a certain way.

We also practice our pick-and-roll defense in our four-on-four shell drill by showing how we want to trap the side pick and roll and our subsequent weak-side rotations. We must stop the ball and force the trapped dribbler high and away from the basket. Our trappers should always try to send the man with the ball back to his original defender.

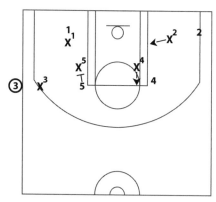

Figure 7.13
SOB defense man to man: we pressure 3 to influence pass to 1 in the corner and body and three-quarters 1. X^5 stops 5 from screening down. X^4 overplays 4 and X^2 sloughs off of 2 until ball is unbounded. We want to stop ball reversal.

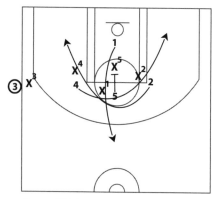

Figure 7.14
SOB defense man to man—late clock (under seven seconds): switch everything once the ball has been inbounded or whenever players cross with or without the ball. We also want to stand up screeners. We have inverted X^1 and X^5.

Our interceptors are taught to read the eyes of the player being trapped to anticipate where he might pass. We want our player to be in position to possibly steal the pass thrown out of the trap. Our trappers are told to influence any pass made over the trapper's outside shoulder. We always want to eliminate the penetrating or gut pass that places us in a difficult scramble situation. Interceptors must know which offensive players are the stronger outside threats, players who we must close out on; on poorer shooters we can bump back to stop basket penetration.

We constantly remind our players that we want to gang rebound defensively and keep our opponents and the ball out of the middle of the court.

Players must be aware of their own individual ability and speed when trapping. Some players can quickly trap from two or three steps away and others can rapidly cover distance from four or five strides away. When trapping, it is very important to create indecision on the part of the offense by repeatedly feinting and faking the trap. We always want to turn our opponent's primary ball handler so that our closest off-the-ball defenders can blindside him or

Figure 7.15
SOB defense wild card—triangle and two: we topside 1 and 2 and overplay 5 with X^3. X^5 and X^4 protect the goal and are in position to double 1 and 2 and prevent the slice cut by 3.

attack and double-team him from behind. We have a special numbering system to call this defensive tactic.

Terminology and communication are also very important if you want to play good defense. Don't take it for granted that your players grasp and understand everything you talk about. Ask questions to make sure your players understand what you are demanding.

Out-of-Bounds Defense

Diagram your SOB (side out of bounds) and BOB (baseline out of bounds) defenses. Explain your man-to-man, straight zone, switching off of the inbounds passer, and combination zone defense with a wild card defender in the middle. The wild card defender can be the inbound passer's man, your best interceptor or anticipator, or a big man. Explain and walk through each different scenario. You can switch everything straight up and/or invert and then switch everything. Explain how you want to defend late- or short-clock situations. You may want to trap the first pass and deny everything or force apparent receivers backdoor. You must have great ball pressure if you

Figure 7.16
BOB defense: X^3 protects the middle and pressures the ball or zones up. X^1 and X^2 come together and switch. X^4 bodies up and X^5 stops dive by 4 or 2. If X^5 steps out, X^3 and X^5 can call a switch.

Figure 7.17
BOB defense: X^4 takes the corner pass to 1. X^5 takes away dive by 4 or 5. As X^3 helps X^2 cover weak-side. If 3 steps in to receive pass, X^4 and X^1 trap the ball.

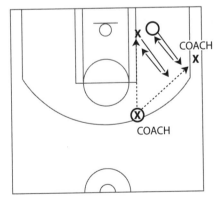

Figure 7.18
Individual defense: deny, overplay, snap back, and touch pass with the defender's outside hand and then repeat by denying back from wing to low-post area and tipping the pass with the hand nearest the basket.

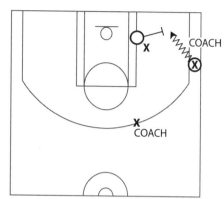

Figure 7.19

Front the post and double the baseline drive: once we tip the ball on the low post, we have the defender front the post by sitting on the post man's legs, and then we have him front the baseline drive.

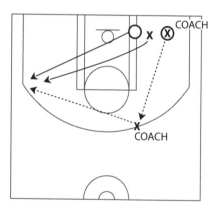

Figure 7.20

After we trap the baseline drive, we pass coach to coach and have the defender close out and play one on one with the original offensive player.

want your overplays to be effective. You should have a signal or predetermined call for each defensive option in case you decide to vary your out-of-bounds defense during the game. The amount of time on the shot or game clock might very well influence which defense you play (Figures 7.13, 7.14, 7.15, 7.16, and 7.17).

Individual Defensive Drills

Figures 7.18 through 7.20 show individual wing denial, post defense, doubling the baseline drive, and close-out drills.

Woodson's Weak-Side Defensive Scheme

Mike Woodson is an outstanding former NBA player who spent eight years as an assistant coach in the league. We both aided and helped the Detroit Pistons win the 2004 NBA Championship. Mike has moved on to a head-coaching job with the Atlanta Hawks, and I have gone with him as an assistant coach. Woodson feels that whenever the ball is on one side of the court and you are defending an isolation play, a screen and roll, cross screen, or post-up, your weak-side defenders must cover certain areas of the court. His key terms are the nail, elbows, and boxes, depending on whether or not the opposition is running an isolation or a two-man play.

On isolations, Woodson believes you can force either sideline or toward the middle as long as you have the near box and near elbow covered by defenders. No matter which direction we force the dribbler, the defender knows there are always teammates waiting to help him. We constantly work on this concept in practice, reminding our players of their responsibility to execute the right way. We believe our weak-side defenders have the responsibility to see their man and the ball at all times. We also prefer to force the isolated offensive player uphill and away from the basket and toward our help. Our goal is to shrink the court to provide help in our team defense.

8

Defending the Pick and Roll

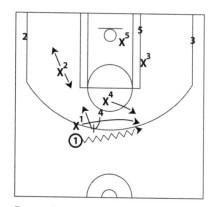

Figure 8.1
High screen and roll: zone up and go under. Strong side is filled.

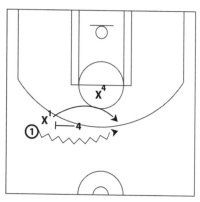

Figure 8.2
Early drag screen and roll: above 3-point line big plays centerfield and zones up. Guard goes under and through. With the shorter 3-point line in college and international basketball we might want to vary our pick-and-roll coverage.

Two-man plays are often referred to as pick and rolls or screen and rolls. The pick and roll occurs quickly and in many different areas of the court causing different players to adjust to defend different situations instantaneously. Your pick-and-roll defense must be consistent and constantly practiced. This chapter contains explanations of the different ways we defend each pick-and-roll situation.

Different Types of Pick and Rolls

We believe in establishing a solid defensive foundation. We then can modify and intensify our method of defending the pick and roll during a game if we are having difficulty stopping an opponent. We always know our personnel and factor in their abilities when deciding how to go about defending a particular play. We do not vary our defensive basics. We play the pick and roll the way we normally do because we believe strongly in our players' abilities and in how we defend particular plays. I have read that the most difficult play to defend in all of basketball was the screen and roll, and I definitely agree.

High Pick and Rolls

Many times the screener comes up through the nail in the middle of the free-throw lane so the defensive player guarding the ball doesn't know which side the screen is coming from. It is imperative that the screener's defender talks and lets his teammate know a screen is going to be set. If the screen is set above the three-point line we normally contact show with our big man who then steps back to let the dribbler's defender slide through and in front to help him beat his opponent to the spot to stop penetration. If the screen is set inside the three-point line we normally fight our way over the screen and have the man guarding the screener step out aggressively to stop the ball and any dribble penetration. In late-clock situations we would not be reluctant to switch either of these pick-and-roll plays, and many times we decide beforehand to switch if equal-size players are involved in any screen and rolls or any other two-man plays. At times we will go through and have our big man drop back and zone up or trap the ball to stop penetration, then drop back into a two-three zone. If the player guarding the ball plays nose-to-nose and hard on the ball with his opponent we feel he won't run into screens and we will then be able to stop the effectiveness of the pick and roll. Stopping the effectiveness of the pick and roll is a matter of the effort and determination of the defender on the ball. See Figures 8.1, 8.2, 8.3, and 8.4.

Double High-Post Elbow Area Pick and Rolls (Rolls, Dives, Quick Slips by the Screener, Pop-Backs, Rescreens, and Fades)

The screener's defender steps out to stop the ball as the dribbler's defender fights over the screen. If the

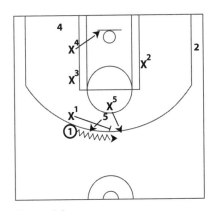

Figure 8.3
Trap high pick and roll: stop the ball.

Figure 8.4
Sending the high pick and roll toward the dribbler's weak hand or away from the screen: X^5 zones up in centerfield. X^1 forces 1 weak. X^2 helps and recovers.

Figure 8.5
On the double high elbow or wing pick and roll, X^1 goes over the first screen and under the second as X^5 jumps out to stop the ball.

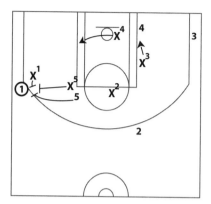

Figure 8.6
Force wing pick and roll uphill and trap with X¹ and X⁵. X² and X⁴ are interceptors. X³ is the goaltender.

screener rolls we will rotate big to big and have the weak-side elbow defensive player beat the other big man to the spot inside the lane while the screener's defender sprints to pick up any unguarded weak-side offensive player stepping out to position himself for a jump-shot opportunity. Our nearest weak-side wing player must be in a position to help on the big man popping out if his teammate is late getting there. We can also decide to aggressively trap the dribbler with the screener's defender. To prevent the screener from slipping to the goal before the screen is set we must try to stay inside and maintain contact with the screener.

Figure 8.7
Force wing pick and roll middle—hard show and X¹ goes under.

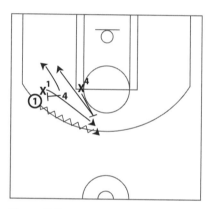

Figure 8.8
Force wing pick and roll middle. Go under and through screener's defender.

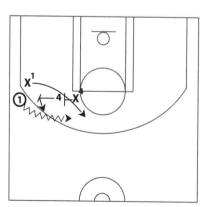

Figure 8.9
Force wing pick and roll middle and squeeze or hug the screener as X¹ goes under.

Figure 8.10
5 sets screen for 1, and X⁵ hugs screener. X¹ goes under the screen to stop 1.

Repicks

Most teams rescreen when the on-the-ball defender goes under both the screener and his defender on a pick and roll. We will use this defensive tactic when we feel the dribbler is not a good perimeter shooter but is a very dangerous penetrator. Defensively, if the dribbler and screener recognize this, the screener sets another screen for the dribbler as he changes direction to again use the screen. When this happens we teach the screener's defender to jump out and aggressively trap the ball, turning the dribbler back to his defender. We want to "blitz" or "red" the dribbler. We want both of our defenders to come together to stop the dribbler from splitting the defensive switch or trap. In late- or short-clock situations we switch all pick and rolls regardless of the player's size differences (Figure 8.11).

Single-Elbow Pick and Rolls

The defender on the dribbler must body up and fight over the screen; the screener's defender either contact shows to stop the ball, traps the ball, or zones up to stop penetration. The defense must stop penetration and the straight-line drive because many teams

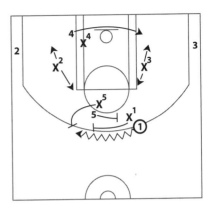

Figure 8.11

1 reverses direction as 5 comes back to screen X^1. X^5 and X^1 trap 1, and X^2 and X^3 are in position to pick up 5 if he pops or dives.

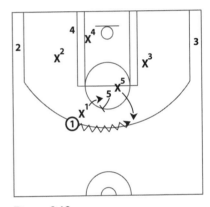

Figure 8.12

In late-clock or end-of-game situations we switch X^1 and X^5 regardless of size and try to force the dribbler uphill or toward our help.

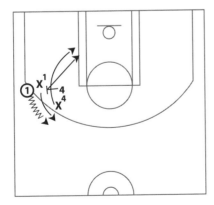

Figure 8.13

Force the wing pick and roll middle but 4 slips to the goal. X^4 must stay connected to and inside 4.

have the corner vacated to take away the help on this offensive maneuver (Figure 8.15).

Wing or Side Pick and Rolls

We can play these screens a number of ways, but our primary defense is to fight our way over the screen, with the screener's defender stepping out to stop ball

Figure 8.14
Hard show and over: X⁴ shows hard to trap and stop the ball with X¹. X⁵ rotates early to 4, and X⁴ rotates to 5.

Figure 8.15
X⁵ traps I with X¹ as X¹ fights over the screen set by 5. X⁴ picks up 5 if he rolls, and X² picks up 5 if he pops out.

Figure 8.16
Force wing pick and roll sideline. Screen pops and is not a shooter. Weak-side players help and recover and stay with their individual opponents.

Figure 8.17
This is the rotation when we force wing pick and roll sideline and the screener dives.

penetration and enable the dribbler's defender to catch up to and stop his man. We expect to get help from the nail or plug man and we are relying on weak-side rotation should the offensive screener fade to the near sideline or short corner. In the latter case we can prerotate early big to big (Figure 8.14). At times we will decide to force the wing pick and roll sideline if the near side corner is filled. We use a special signal when we want to force sideline when the corner is filled. Again, in short-clock situations we will switch regardless of size.

Defend the slip move on the side pick and roll as if it was an isolation play. As shown in Figure 8.19, the player guarding the screener (X^4) must stay inside and attached to his man to front and take away the inside cut. Weak-side defenders X^2, X^3, and X^5 must cover the nail, elbow, and box. We want to force the isolated offensive player uphill and away from the basket to our help. We are almost defending this in our shadow or tilt defense.

Corner Screen and Rolls

We prefer to force sideline to trap the corner pick and roll. It is imperative that we front the post and have the elbows and boxes covered to provide weak side help (Figure 8.20).

Figure 8.18
Here we force wing pick and roll sideline and trap the dribbler as 4, a shooter, pops back.

Figure 8.19
Defending a slip move on side pick and roll, X^4 must stay attached and get inside the screener.

Figure 8.20
Corner pick and roll: trap the ball.

Figure 8.21
Defend drag pick and roll: X⁴ must play centerfield to help guide X¹ under the transition screen.

Figure 8.22
The reverse pick and roll when a small player sets a screen on the wing. X¹ switches while X⁴ forces 4 uphill. We can also trap the ball and rotate.

Random and Early or Transition Pick and Rolls and Weak-Side Defense and Rotations

We normally find these pick and rolls difficult to trap; therefore we instruct the screener's defender to zone up and try to stop penetration to help the dribbler's defender instead of aggressively trapping the ball. Talk and communication are necessary as is having all our defenders hustling back to get level with the ball to be in position to stop penetration. Many coaches refer to random pick and rolls as the drag play (Figure 8.21).

Reverse Pick and Roll

In this situation smaller players screen bigger players on the point of the ball in the high elbow area, the low post, or the short corner. We generally try to aggressively switch or trap this unconventional pick and roll. We rely on weak-side help from the nail and elbow and boxes and will front should the screener roll to the low post on a mismatch (Figure 8.22).

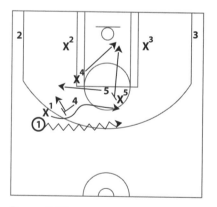

Figure 8.23
Staggered high double pick and roll with X⁴ picking up 5 rotating and X⁵ rotating to 4.

Multiple or Staggered High Screens on the Ball

We usually fight over the first screen and under or through the second screen. At times we might also switch up the line with the highest defender involved in the screens. We also will alert our weak-side defenders beforehand if we decide to play on the top-side of the player receiving the screen, forcing him away from the staggered double. We feel this may negate the effectiveness of the multiple or staggered screen; many times it will also have the added bonus of frustrating the offensive player. The two defensive players guarding the two players setting the double screens set themselves up in tandem so that they can cover a greater area and bump or impede the progress of the offensive player who is using the screen until the defender can corral him (Figure 8.23).

When defending the successive high center field double pick and roll and the successive double-wing pick and roll, we want the player guarding the second screener to trap or show hard on the ball. This permits the player guarding the dribbler to go under the screen to get to the ball and stop penetration (Figure 8.24).

To summarize our pick-and-roll defense, we practice and drill against these defensive schemes regularly and work on our calls, signals, and tactics. You should be consistent, teaching your players to react instantly and instinctively to situations so they won't have to think about how to cover a specific offensive maneuver or tactic. Encourage your players to react instinctively. Don't let them think about what they have to do!

Your players should also learn how to defend direct inside point-of-the-ball screens for a post player on the elbow, low block, pinch post, and wing: In this screening situation we aggressively switch the screen, and we expect to provide weak-side help by covering the nail, elbow, and boxes (Figure 8.25).

Sometimes on a predetermined signal we will have the player guarding the screener step in front

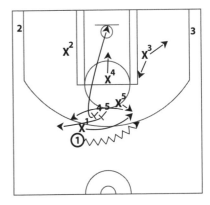

Figure 8.24
Double centerfield high pick and roll: X^1 tries to fight over both screens as X^4 and X^5 play tandem defense. X^4 picks up the big who rolls and X^5 gets the other big after he has stopped the ball.

Figure 8.25
5 screens 4, and X^5 and X^4 switch. We switch this low-post screen in most instances regardless of size.

Figure 8.26
We again switch X¹ and X⁴, and X² is ready to rotate from the nail to 1 fading out to the sideline.

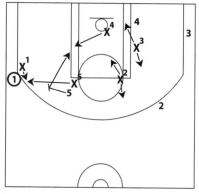

Figure 8.27
X⁵ traps the ball before 5 sets his screen and 1 is able to break the defense down or split our pick-and-roll defense.

of the player he is guarding and aggressively trap the ball before the screen can be set.

We use predetermined verbal or visual signals to differentiate how we cover each specific pick-and-roll situation. Many teams use colors or key words to describe the defense they want to use at a specific time. Some teams might want to use the color Red to describe trapping the dribbler in the high or side pick and roll as well as the tactic they use to defend a sideline step-up. *Weak* might be the term they use to designate forcing the dribbler away from the high pick and roll or side pick and roll his weak hand. *Sideline* might describe forcing the side pick and roll down the sideline toward the baseline instead of uphill and away from the basket (Figures 8.26 and 8.27).

Rules for Defending Pick and Rolls

Always try to take something away from the offense. Don't let them run what they have practiced. Unless our intent is to force the dribbler sideline on a pick and roll, we always emphasize forcing the dribbler uphill and away from the basket to stop penetration whether or not we are trapping the ball. Here are some tactics that we use:

1. Trap the dribbler and go over the screen.
2. Hard show and over.
3. Hard show and through one man removed. At times we use this tactic and then fall back into a two-three zone once we have stopped the ball.
4. Pinch, squeeze, or push up and under or through.
5. Trap and aggressively switch the rescreen to take something away from the offense.
6. Jump and trap the dribbler early before the screen can be set.

7. Defend the roll man with a big-to-big rotation. Always be aware of covering the nail (plug), elbow, and box on the weak side. These defenders are drawn to the ball on the dribble or pass to shrink the floor.

8. Defend the pop-back man.

9. Switch the pick and roll; you can always switch equal-size players.

10. Late clock: Three-point line strategy— switch at all times—force the offense to adjust.

11. NBA shadow or tilt principle with weak-side zone help.

Wing or Side Pick and Roll

Do you show and go under, fight over with help, jump the dribbler before the screen is set (run and jump action), show hard and go through, string the dribbler out, squeeze and go under, trap the ball, or have the big man sag off the screener and let the dribbler's defender go in front of him as he zones up and plays centerfield to stop penetration and clog the middle? These are all pick-and-roll defensive schemes. You must decide which you want to teach and use. Which of these best suits your philosophy and personnel? Emphasize how the nail or plug man must be able to help immediately to stop the ball when the dribbler comes off the screen.

If we sideline the wing pick and roll, the defender on the dribbler turns the ball down and forces him toward the nearest sideline by getting on the high side on his inside shoulder to force him away from the screen. The defender on the screener drops off the screener toward the basket to help corral straight-line drives to the basket and to be prepared to stop the ball and trap it at the baseline hash mark.

If the screener pops back, we cover him with our nearest perimeter defender playing the elbow, plug, or nail position. This defender's aggressiveness is determined by whether or not the screener is a threat

Figure 8.28
Force wing pick and roll sideline.

as a jump shooter. We prefer to stop the ball and help and recover, faking a rotation if possible, in case a pass is made. If the screener is not a shooter, his original defender will rotate back to him once the pass is made.

If the screener dives, the elbow or plug man steps over to force him behind to take away his inside cut. In this case the weak-side big man crosses the lane and picks up the dive man at the dotted line in front of the basket. The weak-side wing defender must rotate back to protect the goal and get inside the low-post player. If the dribbler passes out to the top or weak side, all defenders are responsible for recovering to their own men while the ball is in the air, not after the catch.

If we turn the ball sideline and decide to trap the dribbler we must seal the trap and not let the dribbler split the defenders to get to the middle of the court. We aggressively trap the ball as soon as the screener sets the screen to stop the dribbler from penetrating down the sideline and turning the corner to the basket area.

If we force the sideline pick and roll toward the middle, not to the sideline, we either make a hard show and go under or aggressively fight over the screen and trap to stop the ball. When we trap the ball and stop it we are in a defensive alignment where our next nearest defenders on either side of the trappers with the trappers in front of them are our interceptors, and the defender farthest from the ball is our high or low goaltender (depending on the position of the ball). Our goaltender always has two trappers and two interceptors in front of him.

In each defensive scheme we use, we want to take away basket penetration and the offense's ability to get the ball from one side of the court to the other. The screener on the ball slides under the screener to recover to his man in the first instance and fights over the screen and stays with his man in the second. The screener's defender makes a hard show as the dribbler comes off the screen, forcing him farther out on the perimeter, and then recovers to the roll man when we go through the screen. If we are going over the screen the screener's defender goes with his man and makes a hard right-angle show as the dribbler comes off of the screen, forcing him to pick up his dribbler or to dribble away from the goal, higher out on the floor. Once either of these things is accomplished, the screener's defender quickly recovers to the roll man.

We can also hug or squeeze to have the defender on the dribbler force his man toward the screen and then slide under both the screener and his teammate to get to his man to stop penetration. The screener's defender bodies up and forces the screen as high as possible while staying attached to his man. If the offense repicks when we squeeze and go under, we automatically and aggressively trap the repick.

Basic Philosophy of How to Defend the Pick and Roll

When defending pick and rolls on the wing and in the center of the court, we must decide on whether to hard show and go under, stop the ball and go over, jump out to stop the ball and go through, squeeze the screener and go under, jump the screen before it is set, or trap the dribbler with the big man turning the dribbler back to his defender. On repicks when the dribbler's defender goes underneath the screen, we teach our big men to trap the ball. At times we will switch the pick and roll when similar-size players are involved. We will also sideline the wing area pick and roll. We have also experimented with trapping the corner pick and roll and forcing the ball to the corner or baseline area so we can employ our two-two-one trapping zone. We may also hard trap the elbow pick and roll when the ball is at the top of the key. We have different verbal signals for each of these defensive maneuvers. It is important to remem-

Figure 8.29
V set fights over the screen; X⁴ and X⁵ rotate big to big.

ber that you make the decision as to how you want to play the screen and roll and that you avoid saddling your players with choices that might confuse them. We believe in teaching one standard defense first to perfect that tactic. We feel we can then teach our team how to adjust and change if our standard defensive scheme is not functioning properly.

Double-High Elbow Pick and Roll

Figure 8.29 demonstrates how we hard show and fight over on the double-high elbow pick and roll with the opposite big man helping in lane, how we stay home on strong-side wing, slough off of and help off of weak-side wing to act as an interceptor or goaltender.

Responsibility of the Player Defending the Screener

Make certain the big man knows his job. Prevent confusion and indecision. When defending the pick and roll the player guarding the screener is responsible for stopping dribble penetration and preventing the ball from getting from one side of the court to the other. Once he steps out to stop the ball, the defender must quickly recover to his man and by using his arms pressure and force him to receive a lob rather than a bounce or direct pass. To defend against a screener slipping to the goal the defender must stay attached to and inside the player setting the screen to deny the inside cut and post up.

UCLA Set: Pick-and-Roll Drill

Show and under on wing pick and roll, show and under on high pick and roll, and trap wing pick and roll on the weak side (live) with full rotation (big to big). Force the dribbler up hill. (For a graphic representation of this defense, see Figures 5.40, 5.41, 5.42, and 5.43.)

Reverse Pick and Roll

Another difficult maneuver to defend is the reverse screen and roll where the smaller offensive player comes to set an on-the-ball screen on a bigger defender. This places the smaller player in the position of having to stop and possibly defend a bigger and stronger offensive player out on the perimeter or in the low post in an area he is probably not accustomed to defending.

Teams occasionally show and recover and then zone up versus the pick and roll in the center of the court at the top of the key area. Teams have been known to trap any corner pick and rolls as well as the repick of any screen-and-roll maneuver. We will trap and/or switch any repicks, which usually occur when the defender guarding the ball handler goes under the defender whose man sets the screen; the dribbler reverses his path and goes back the other way, enabling the original screener to get another shot at screening the dribbler's defender to free the man with the ball.

Defend the drag pick and roll by having the screener's defender zone up instead of aggressively attacking the dribbler because this usually happens in transition and it is difficult to stay connected to the screener. Our objective is to stop penetration and then level back even with the ball.

Figures 8.26 to 8.31 show the rotations used to defend and call out the high pick and roll play with the weak side both filled and empty.

Sideline Pick-and-Roll Defense

If and when you decide to sideline or force the pick and roll away from the screen, your players must understand that verbal communication is a key to defending this maneuver. If the defender guarding the man in the corner yells, "corner filled" or another key term you may want to use, he will have alerted his teammates to the fact that he is in the cor-

Figure 8.30
We zone up with X^4 and X^1 and fall back into a 2-3 zone. Whenever the opportunity presents itself, we will rotate X^4 to the backline of the defense and bring X^2 or X^3 up to the top.

Figure 8.31
X^4 zones up as X^1 goes beneath the screen set by X^4.

Figure 8.32
Wing pick and roll: hard show or trap
by X⁴ on 1. X⁵ anticipates the roll by 4
and rotates early, crosses the lane, and
defends 4. All other defenders rotate
according to the pass.

ner defensively to help out should the dribbler try to make a quick move to the basket along the sideline. Hearing this verbal signal also alerts players defending the pick and roll that they can force the ball toward the sideline where they'll have strong-side help. The goal is always to stop the ball when defending all pick and rolls. Penetration destroys your defense and sets up draw-and-kick opportunities that are difficult to defend and cause you to scramble and rotate. Our pick-and-roll defense is designed to stop the offense from reversing the basketball and to force them to pick up the ball.

Elbow Pick-and-Roll Defense

We caution our players to try and trap the elbow pick and roll because we must stop the ball and any subsequent dribble penetration. We don't want to permit the offense to split the double team or trap. Stop the penetrating outlet pass. Force the offense to throw the ball outside to enable teammates to recover to their men and rotate properly.

Double-High-Wing Pick-and-Roll Defense

When defending the double-high-wing pick and roll, we want the player guarding the dribbler to fight over the first screen, go under the second screen, and beat his man to the spot. We must stop the ball and basket penetration.

We have also experimented with aggressively trapping the high pick and roll in the center of the court and then falling back into a two-three zone once the dribbler has passed the ball back to the fading (or stepping back) screener. We defend this by rotating our weak-side wing up to guard the screener, while having the other two weak-side defenders form a line across the basket area while the trapper rotates back to the goal or the now strong side baseline area. The trapper reads the open area and goes to defend the open offensive player in that spot. In the NBA, which uses a shorter shot clock, this is an effective defensive maneuver, but I think it will also be successful in any level of basketball. Certainly it will change the tempo and cause the offense to react in a different way.

Staggered Drag Pick-and-Roll Defense

When defending the drag double-high or elbow-staggered screen it is imperative that the man guarding the second screener stay connected so that he can stop or trap dribble penetration. The first screener can let the man guarding the defender through and then shrink to the middle of the lane to pick up the roll man, if necessary.

Figure 8.33
Force wing pick and roll sideline to initiate our baseline trap and rotations (screener pops).

Summary of Pick-and-Roll Defensive Strategy

Pick-and-roll defense requires your players to force the dribbler away from the goal. Your team's mind-set must be to stop penetration. The screener's defender has a tremendous responsibility in these situations. When teaching defending the wing, high, or elbow pick and roll, we always begin by asking the dribbler's defender to belly or body up to the man with the ball and fight to get over the screen by making himself thinner. The defender on the ball must be physical, and the defender guarding the screener must contact show and step out to stop the ball from being reversed to the other side of the floor.

When defending the wing or side pick and roll, many teams aggressively show or softly double-team the ball until they have successfully stopped dribble penetration. They then rotate according to the flight of the ball. If the ball is advanced or kicked ahead, across the floor to the weak side they usually recover back to their own men. However, when the ball is

Figure 8.34
Force wing pick and roll sideline with the rotation on skipped pass to 2 from 1.

kicked back to the screener and/or stays on the strong side of the court, they will usually rotate early and aggressively from the closest weak-side big man (Figures 8.32–8.34).

Defending the two-man pick and roll is probably the most difficult defensive maneuver your players have to contend with. Coaches must continually work diligently with their players to teach them how to stop this play (Figures 8.35–8.38).

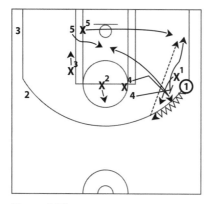

Figure 8.35
Wing defends the screen and roll with the strong side empty when not forcing sideline.

Figure 8.36
Defending the high pick and roll with the strong side empty when not forcing sideline. If X^4 cannot get back to 4 popping out, X^5 must sprint and prerotate. We can also immediately tilt or shadow X^5.

Figure 8.37
Transition drag and step-up screen and rolls. Big on small guard fights over the screen.

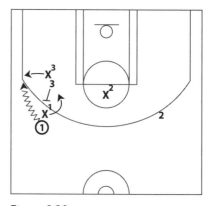

Figure 8.38
Step up pick and roll. Switch similar size 3 and 1.

Defending Specific Plays

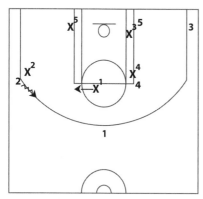

9

Figure 9.1
Defending the wing: isolation is by shadowing or tilting and covering nail boxes and elbow once 2 has the ball. X^2 tries to force 2 to his help. We want 2 to give up the ball.

Figure 9.2
Trapping the isolation on the wing: X^1 and X^2 are trappers, X^3 and X^5 are interceptors, and X^4 is deep goaltender. (X^3 and X^4 invert if possible.)

In this chapter, we will diagram and discuss defense against post-ups and/or isolations. (How we defend the pick and roll on all areas of the court as well as and all other on-the-ball screens is covered in Chapter 8.) We want to play the isolated player one on one, and we want to keep him in front of our help defenders. If we need to, we provide weak-side-help defense with aggressive pressure coming from the plug or nail man and from the weak side (elbow and nail). We may also employ the NBA Shadow and Tilt format or Mike Woodson's suggested elbow and boxes help defense principles. (See Figures 9.1 and 9.2, as well as "Woodson's Weak-Side Defensive Scheme" in Chapter 7.)

When defending players split or cross after entering the ball to the post, it is important for the men guarding those players to come together to prevent them from splitting the defense and cutting to the goal. In this manner your defenders can also come together and switch defensive assignments to stop penetration and easy backdoor cuts. When switching, it is also important that we aggressively force the offense back uphill and take something away from them.

Defending Offensive Maneuvers and Specific Plays

One of our major points of emphasis when defending is to pressure the ball to make passing difficult. This is a tactic we use for defending every play discussed in this chapter.

Cross Screen. When defending the cross screen we want to body up to the player receiving the screen to force him to go from low to high. In this way we stay attached to keep him from receiving the ball on the low block, as shown in Figure 9.3. We can also prevent having to switch a smaller man on a bigger player, which eliminates the chance of a low-post mismatch. On big-on-big and small-on-big horizontal cross screens (single and double) we again believe in bodying up and forcing uphill the player receiving the screen. Many teams, however, have the screener's defender bump the man receiving the screen while his defender goes under the screen and beats him to a spot above the low block. Other teams will ride the screener low and force him toward the baseline and out of bounds. In some instances, we also believe in switching big to big when defending high big-to-big cross screens. One cross-screen maneuver that is difficult to defend—and one we work on continually—is when the screener gets a running start and rapidly runs to set a screen on the ball from the opposite baseline, the weak-side basket area on the wing, the baseline or low baseline area up to the high-post, elbow, or wing areas, as shown in Figure 9.4. It is difficult for the screener's defender to quickly follow his man when the screener sprints from a stationary position to set an on-the-ball screen. When this occurs, we sometimes have to zone up, talk, and help the defensive player guarding the screener over the screen while trying to stop the ball.

Flex Cut. When defending the flex offense baseline cut, we prefer to body up, ride, and force the cutter low and out of bounds to take him out of the play. By doing this we can also stay attached to the screener to stop him from stepping in, sealing his defender, and posting up in the lane after the cut is made. When teams have a big man flex cut off of another big man we aggressively switch the cut and take away the offense's post-up opportunity. Another maneuver you can use to defend a cross screen or a weak-side cut or dive across the lane to the post is to butt screen the offensive player before he gets to his position and not allow him to cut inside and across your face. Force him backdoor or make him change

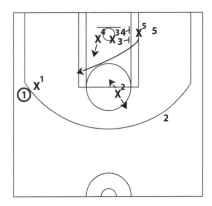

Figure 9.3
Defending the double-cross screen: X^3 and X^4 play horizontal helping tandem defense while X^5 bodies up to and forces 5 from low to high. X^2 covers the nail and 2. X^1 pressures and forces 1 uphill.

Figure 9.4
The cross screen: 5 has a running start as 1 screens. X^1 tries to hold 5 up until X^5 can get over the screen. X^2 plays the nail. X^3 plays the weak-side box.

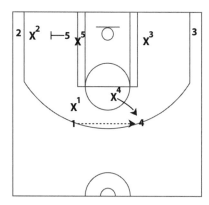

Figure 9.5
The flex cut A: X^1 pressures the ball, X^4 plays the nail and then moves on the pass to 4. X^5 three-quarters 5 on the post. X^3 plays the weak side.

Figure 9.6
The flex cut B: X^4 pressures 4. X^2 bodies and forces 2 from high to low. X^5 denies 5 post-up position. X^1 supports and plays nail. X^3 helps X^2 and covers next pass to 3.

his path to the post. The defender on the ball must be pressured. He must not be allowed to make an uncontested entry pass (Figures 9.5 and 9.6).

UCLA Vertical Post Cut. How the player guards the cutter's route depends on whether or not the cutter is a low-post threat. We will body up and definitely ride the cutter over the screen if he is a low-post threat. We might go below the screen and take a shortcut if we want to take away the cutter's options and not let him use a baseline single or double screen on the other side of the court. We don't want to give offensive players a choice (Figures 9.7 and 9.8).

Utah Diagonal Up Screen from the Baseline. The screener's defender calls out the screen and the defender guarding the recipient of the screen bodies up, rides, and forces his opponent over the screen and away from the basket. We caution the defender guarding the screener not to chase the back picker, get too close to him, and pick off his own teammate. We want him to be in a position to bump, step out, and hold up the cutter (Figure 9.9).

Hawk Cut. In the same way we defend the UCLA cut, the route of the cutter's defender depends on

Figure 9.7
UCLA cut: X^1 bodies up and forces 1 over the top of screen by 5 as X^5 helps X^4 and X^3 cover the weak-side elbow and box.

whether or not the cutter is a low-post threat. We also caution the defender guarding the dribbler to force his man uphill so the ball cannot be entered to the cutter posting up once the cut has been made (Figure 9.10).

Step-Ups or Open-Court Back Screens In this defensive move, we try to trap the dribbler using the screen, or we aggressively switch it and force the dribbler back uphill and away from the basket. We want to switch the step-up back pick and flare with all three defenders involved—especially in a late-game or short-clock situation (Figure 9.11).

Diagonal Back Screens. We body up forcing the cutter to take a high path. The players (the diagonal back picks may be single or double) guarding the screeners bump to stand up or hold up the player receiving the screen. Again, we don't want to chase the back picker and screen our own teammate (Figure 9.12).

Jam or Flare Screens. We close the distance and body up to the player receiving the screen. The screener's defender tries to help by screening the screener or by faking at the flaring player to hold

Figure 9.8
UCLA cut: once 5 has the ball, X^5 tries to pressure and stop ball reversal. X^3 topsides 3 on a wide pindown as X^4 tries to stand up 4 before he can get a screen. X^1 either fronts or three-quarters 1.

Figure 9.9
Utah diagonal up screen: 2 sets an up screen for 4 as X^4 bodies up and forces 4 over the screen and away from the post. X^2 helps and does not chase the screener and pick off his own teammate.

Figure 9.10
Hawk cut: X^2 bodies up to 2 and forces him over the screen set by 4 as X^4 helps X^5 and X^3 helps on the weak-side box and elbow.

him up. The screener's defender must also be aware of the screener trying to slip and dive to the basket (Figure 9.13).

Figure 9.11
Step-up screen: X³ traps 1 with X¹ if he is close to X³ when screen occurs. If not, X³ plays soft as X¹ fights over. We will also switch step-up flare.

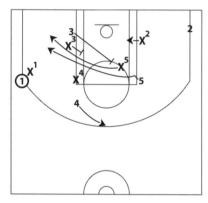

Figure 9.12
Diagonal weak-side back screen: X¹ pressures. X⁵ bodies up to and forces 5 over the screen and off of the low block as X³ helps. X² covers weak-side block, and X⁴ stays level with the ball on the strong-side elbow.

Figure 9.13
Jam or flare screen: X⁴ tries to help as 4 sets a jam screen on X¹ for 1. X¹ must body up to 1 and fight over the screen. X³ can feint and recover to help X¹.

Figure 9.14
Turnouts and curls: X⁴ and X⁵ stand up 4 and 5 as they try to screen down for 3 and 2. X³ rides the hip and outside shoulder to make 3 curl the screen as X⁴ steps out and helps. X¹ drops to the elbow on the pass to stop penetration.

Turnouts and Curls. We try to hold the screener up while the defender on the player receiving the screen locks and trails his opponent and, with the big man's help, gets on his outside shoulder and hip to make him curl the screen. The screener's defender must also contact show to give help. Once the ball is passed to the curling offensive player, the passer's defender must move on the pass and immediately drop back toward the nail to help his teammate and stop any penetration by the curling player. We can also have the player defending the offensive-screen receiver shoot the gap, and have the screener's defender stand the screener up and then step back to let the defender go through in front of him. We will squeeze the screener, or influence the turnout man by giving him only one way to go before he makes his move. The player on the ball must, as previously mentioned, pressure the ball and then immediately drop back to the nail to help on the curl or drive to the middle (Figures 9.14, 9.15, 9.16, and 9.17).

Wide Diagonal Down Screens. As previously explained, we want to stand up the screener and

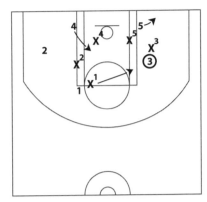

Figure 9.15
Turnouts and curls: in Figure 9.14 X², once he sees the ball passed to 3 on the other side of the court, comes up inside the screen to make 2 fade to the weak-side corner and cuts off his curl to the middle.

Figure 9.16
Turnouts and curls: shooting the gap, 5 sets the screen and X⁵ holds him up, steps back, and lets X² cut in front of him to make 2 fade the screen or force him to catch the ball higher out on the floor.

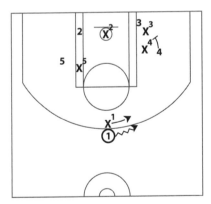

Figure 9.17
Turnouts and curls: X³ topsides 3 taking away his option to cut either across or turn out. Weak-side defenders X⁵ and X² are drawn toward the dribble as X⁴ stands up 4 and X¹ pressures the ball.

Figure 9.18
Wide diagonal down screen: X³ plays topside on 3 as 4 screens down and forces him away from the screen. X¹ pressures 1 on the dribble as X⁵ and X² cover the weak-side elbow and box.

Figure 9.19
Zipper down screen: 4 screens down on X³ to free 3 at the top of the key. X⁴ tries to stand up 4 to permit X³ to go in front of the screen to stop 3 from receiving the pass from 1 or to cause him to receive the ball farther out on the floor.

shortcut this causing the receiver to fade, or we top-side the player receiving the screen and force him baseline (Figure 9.18).

Zipper or Straight Vertical Down Screens. We prefer to stand up the screener and stay attached and try to deny and force the player receiving the screen away or to let him receive the ball and then force him toward the near sideline to stop him from reversing the ball. We don't want to play on top of him with our back to the ball and give him any cutting or step-up options.

Defensively speaking, when you are guarding the player receiving a down screen you should always be moving to slip the screen by moving toward the ball. The ball, once again, should draw you in its direction. Your mind-set should be to never permit yourself to be screened, and to slip inside the screener if possible (Figure 9.19).

Isolations. We either force the isolated offensive player back to the middle (to our plug [nail], elbow, and box defenders) or to the near sideline where we have brought our nearest big defender to provide help (NBA Shadow or Tilt tactic) while occupying the elbows and box with our other three help defend-

Figure 9.20
Isolations: 1 passes to 2 on the wing and cuts away. X² wants to force 2 uphill toward the help.

ers. We prefer to force the isolated offensive player with the ball uphill and toward our help whenever possible (Figures 9.20, 9.21, and 9.22).

Post-Ups. We want to front all post-ups and maintain contact when the ball is extended to the free-throw line or below. We front by sitting on the knees of the posted player to root him off of the post and to protect against the lock and lob. This tactic will also stop the fronted player from jumping to receive a lob pass. Alternatively we might try bodying up and three-quartering the post player if the ball is above the free-throw line. We must have great ball pressure whenever we front the post (Figure 9.23).

Staggered Horizontal, Vertical, or Diagonal Screens. We try to stand up the screeners, bump or body the cutters, and force the players using the screens to go over them if possible. We will have our defender trail on the first screen and go through or shortcut the second screen. At times if the screener's defender is beaten we may switch up the line by having the player guarding the screen receiver call out the switch alerting his defensive teammate to step out and switch (Figure 9.24).

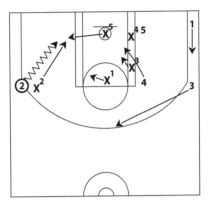

Figure 9.21
Isolations: X^2 forces 2 toward the baseline as X^5 crosses the lane to trap 2 with X^2. X^1, X^3, and X^4 rotate toward the ball to provide weak-side help.

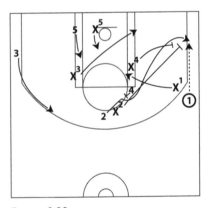

Figure 9.22
Isolations: 2 has ball on the wing after a hawk cut as X^4 traps him form the top with X^2. X^1 and X^3 are interceptors and X^5 is the goaltender.

Figure 9.23
Post-up: X^5 fronts 5, X^1 pressures the ball, X^2 plays the nail, X^4 plays the weak-side box, and X^3 plays the weak-side elbow. X^2 must stop 4 on the nail to stop high-low action.

Weak-Side Cuts Toward the Ball or Strong Side.
To prevent weak-side cuts the defenders must remember that they should be drawn to and stay level with the ball when defending players on the weak side.

Figure 9.24
Staggered screens: X⁴ and X⁵ try to stand up screeners 4 and 5. X⁴ and X⁵ play defense in tandem. X² trails the first screen and, with help from X⁴, cuts in front of X⁴ to deny 2 the ball. If beaten, X² can tell X⁴ to switch up the line.

Figure 9.25
Weak-side cuts to the ball: here X³ loses sight of 3 who cuts behind him to the goal. X³ should be level with the ball to force 3 to cut behind him and away from the goal.

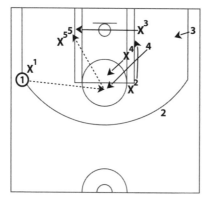

Figure 9.26
High-low defense: X⁵ fronts 5. X¹ pressures the ball. 4 flashes to the high post, and X⁴ must pressure him to make him drive. If 4 passes to 5 in a lock-and-lob situation, X³ must rotate and cross the lane to stop 5. X² sloughs to keep 3 off of the board.

Figure 9.27
Fades: X² tries to shoot the gap on 2's attempted curl. 2 recognizes this and fades. On the pass to 2, X⁵ must close out on 2 on the fade to the corner. X² and other defenders must rotate the ball.

They must keep their opponents away from their bodies and not let them close the distance or cut across their face. If not, they must maintain contact, keep the cutter in front of them or body up, and ride them high. Outstanding peripheral vision is an asset here, as is the ball-you-man principle of defense. A player should not turn his head away from the ball and lose sight of the man he is guarding. Should a player lose sight of the player he is defending, he should open up and retreat to the goal, where the ball will draw him to his man (Figure 9.25).

High-Low Action. Pressure the passer at the high post and play him as if the dribble is used to make him a driver. The post defender must front and sit on the knees of the low-post defender while keeping his hands up. He must stay connected (Figure 9.26).

Fades. When an offensive player fades a turnout or down screen our defender might have to shoot the gap instead of locking and trailing. In this case, the screener's defender might have to switch out to pick up the shooter if his defensive teammate is screened (Figure 9.27).

Pick and Pop. Players must try to stay attached when a screener picks and pops out for a shot. It is easier to stay connected if they can stand up the screener. At times we will squeeze the screener and let the dribbler's defender go under the screen (Figure 9.28).

Feed the Post Cuts. When defending a cutter who has passed to the post, the defender should get level with the ball and his butt to the baseline to keep the cutter in front of him; this will enable him to dig on the post or to force the cutter to the middle where there is weak-side help. We don't want to give the cutter an option. The defender can also take his man to the goal and then snap back to double the post (Figure 9.29).

Figure 9.28
Pick and pop: X¹ is drawn to the ball on the pass from 1 to 2. 1 screens away on X³ and then steps back to the ball. X¹ must help, recover, and step back to stop the pass from 2 to 1.

Figure 9.29
Post feed cuts: on the pass from 1 to 5, X¹ sinks with his butt to the baseline keeping 1 in front of him and only permitting 1 to cut middle where X², X⁴, and X³ are helping on the nail, elbow, and box.

Figure 9.30
Brush screens: 3 drives middle off the cut by 1. X² must full-body show to cause 3 to pass to 2. X⁴ rotates to 2, and X³ picks up 4 if X⁵ cannot pre-rotate and cross the lane in time.

Figure 9.31
Lobs: X⁴ must pressure pass to 4 and then pressure 4 to make him drive. X³ pays half a man on 3 and tries to keep connected and not get above him. X⁵ must see the ball, and X² and X¹ must rotate back to the goal.

Brush Screens. The cutter's or screener's defender must slow down to provide help in case the ball carrier's defender is screened. Our weak-side plug (nail), elbow, and box defenders must see the ball, be drawn to it, and be in position to help if the player with the ball gets a step on his defender (Figure 9.30).

Lobs. Our players try to stay attached and/or keep their opponents in front of them. To prevent the lock and lob we remain connected to the offensive player and guard him on the inside instead of three-quartering. On-the-ball pressure is imperative if we want to successfully defend the lob play.

If we lose sight of our man, we snap back and retreat to the goal with our hands up and in the passing lanes, or we open up and retreat to the goal without losing sight of the ball. Which option you decide to teach is an individual coaching preference, but on-the-ball pressure and weak-side defensive help are always necessary (Figure 9.31).

Horns (Elbow Area) Staggered Double Screens. The defender guarding the cutter can play topside to

Figure 9.32
Horns (elbow area) staggered double screens: X² locks and trails 2 on the first screen by 5 and goes through the second screen by 4. X³ goes to the goal with 3 and tilts back to the box as X¹ plays the nail or elbow and X⁴ and X⁵ play tandem defense in the lane.

force the cutter low below the screens or he can go over the first screen and through on the second, providing the screener's defenders try to step out and slow up the cutter (Figure 9.32).

Dives. Once you have lost sight of your man cutting to the basket when the dribbler drives at you on the perimeter, you either snap back and retreat to the goal or open up, make yourself wide, and retreat to the goal with your hands up (Figure 9.33).

Loops. Our players try to lock and trail by getting on the outside shoulder and hip of the offensive player or they try to play to the inside and turn or force the cutter to the corner or sideline away from the screen (Figure 9.34).

Big-to-Big Diagonal Screen. We normally body up and force the player receiving the screen to cut from low to high. Alternatively we will switch defenders of equal size (Figure 9.35).

Rip or Blind (Back) Screens. We talk and call out the screen. We don't chase the back picker. We may

Figure 9.33
Dives: I dribbles at X⁴ to set up 4's dive to the basket. X⁴ can open up and retreat to the goal in the passing lane or snap back and play the passing lane. X² must be drawn to the ball to help.

Figure 9.34
Loops: X³ locks and trails on 4's screen and goes inside the second screen by 5. X² supports and helps on the weak side.

Figure 9.35
Big-to-big diagonal screens: X⁴ bodies up and forces 4 over the top on the screen by 5. X⁵ helps slow up 4. X² plays the nail and X³ plays the weak-side block. We can switch X⁵ and X⁴ and elbow and box are covered.

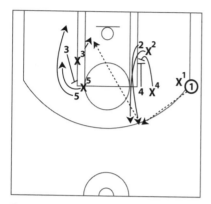

Figure 9.36
Rip or blind back screens: X⁴ tries to hold 4 up. X² plays ball side of 2 and pressures the pass. X³ plays soft on 3's screen. X⁵ bodies up to 5 and fights over the screen. (X⁵ can also slip inside the screen and X³ will bump and hold up 5.)

Figure 9.37
Reverse pick and roll: 4 has the ball on the wing and 1 sets a screen on X⁴. On the small-on-big pick and roll, we have X¹ jump and trap 4's dribble as X⁴ forces 4 uphill. X³ plays the nail and X² stops at the goal to help if 1 rolls and receives a pass.

try to body up and ride the cutter high and away from the basket when we know the screen is coming (Figure 9.36).

Reverse Pick and Roll When a Smaller Player Sets an on-the-Ball Screen for a Taller Player. In this situation we will jump out and aggressively switch and send the dribbler back uphill. Alternatively we may trap aggressively when the players come together (Figure 9.37).

Bonnie or L Cuts. An old-school maneuver or handback where the player passing the ball hands off, takes a couple of steps uphill, and then quickly makes a right-angle cut to the basket. When the cutter cuts high we get below and in front of him and try to pick up the offensive foul as he reverses and cuts to the basket (Figure 9.38).

Blast Cuts. We jump to the ball once a pass to the wing is made so that we can take away inside cuts that can lead to easy baskets. We then try to take away an option and play to the inside to force the cutter to the ball-side corner; or we get on his outside shoulder and force him away from the ball. If he posts up, we front him. Once the cutter goes away

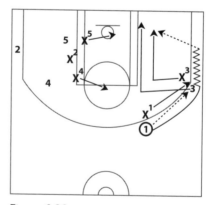

Figure 9.38
Bonnie or L cuts: 1 can pass to 3 and get the ball back or dribble 3 out. On 3's cut X³ gets inside and denies 3 the ball on the right-angle cut to the basket.

we take him to the rim or weak-side foul lane where we can see the ball and look to provide weak-side help (Figure 9.39).

Corner-Filled Situations. In a wing or side pick-and-roll situation with the corner filled, we communicate and force the dribbler sideline where we have help and can possibly trap the ball (Figure 9.40).

Pass and Screen Away Action. On a horizontal pass and screen away we either switch the back man with the man nearest the ball calling the switch or we try to body up and ride the man over the screen (Figure 9.41).

Dribble Handoff. We either go through or inside our teammate whose man passes the ball or we aggressively trap or switch the handoff and send the dribbler back to his defender. At times we might overplay the receiver to force him backdoor (Figure 9.42).

Get Action Where a Player Passes and Follows the Ball for a Return Handoff. We prefer to jump switch and trap this maneuver or we step back to allow the defender whose opponent receives the pass

Figure 9.39
Blast cuts: on the pass to 3, 2 cuts first and X² rides him below the screen by 5. X⁴ supports to prevent the lob pass. On 1's cut X¹ goes insides 5 to cover the cut. X⁵ plays soft on the cuts and then pressures the pass from 3 to 5.

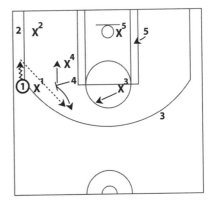

Figure 9.40
Corner-filled situations: we will force the wing pick and roll sideline in the direction of our help. We prevent slips by the screener with this tactic. On pass to 4 popping out, X³ rotates and X⁵ is responsible for pass from 4 to 3.

Figure 9.41
Pass and screen away action: 1 screens away on 2 and we either have X¹ and X² come together and switch or have X¹ step back and permit X² to slide through the screen.

to go through. We do not want him to get screened (Figure 9.43).

Fake the Cross Screen and Pop or Bump Back. We remain attached and stay with the screener while trying to body up and force the player receiving the screen up the lane (Figure 9.44).

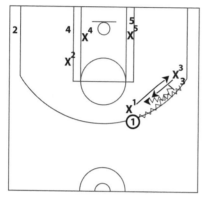

Figure 9.42
Dribble handoff: 1 dribbles to 3 and X¹ steps back to permit X³ to go inside and under the screen to cover 3. We can also aggressively trap and switch this offensive maneuver.

Figure 9.43
Get action pass and return (handback): X¹ and X³ trap the handback and X² is ready to pick up 3 on the cut.

Figure 9.44
Fake cross screen and bump back: X² can topside 2 on the bump back and front and force 2 to the corner, or he can play ballside and take away the bump-back option. X¹ must apply ball pressure.

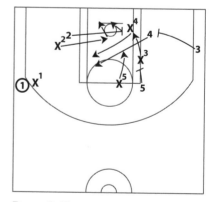

Figure 9.45
Baseline cross screen: 2 sets screen on X⁴ and X⁴ bodies up and forces 4 high to take away low-post option. X² helps and tries to force 2 weak side.

Baseline Cross Screen. We normally switch big-to-big cross screens; when a smaller player screens for a bigger player we stay connected and body up to the player receiving the screen, forcing him from low to high. We also apply as much on-the-ball pressure as possible making it difficult to enter the ball (Figure 9.45).

Pistol Action. This is a maneuver for multiple high point-of-ball screens (step up and jam screen action for the screener). If at all possible we want to switch these screens especially in short- or late-clock situations. If we don't switch the second screen we want to body up and ride the screener over the second screen while applying tough pressure on the player with the ball (Figure 9.46).

Get Hand-Back and Flare Action We will switch as we do in the Pistol action or body up and fight over the jam or flare screen. We might even trap the hand-back if we know it is coming (Figure 9.47).

Misdirection Action. The screener's defender must call out the screen and body the cutter to slow him down while the cutter's defender forces his man from high to low (Figure 9.48).

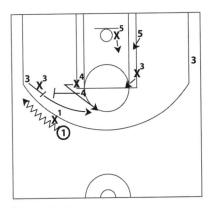

Figure 9.46
Pistol action: we like to trap and jump switch this maneuver or have X³ fight over the screen set by 4.

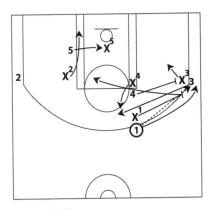

Figure 9.47
Get hand-back and flare: on the 3-to-1 hand-back we will switch X¹ and X³ and then switch X⁴ and X³ on the jam or flare screen. At times we will trap the hand-back and have X⁴ pick up X³ on the flare as X² and X⁵ help.

Figure 9.48
Misdirection action: 3 back picks 2 and then looks to post up. X² must hold up 3 until X³ has gotten on the inside and forced 3 off the low block.

Figure 9.49
Double doubles: X^4 and X^5 stand up screeners 4 and 5 as X^2 locks and trails. X^1 drops into the slot on the pass to 2. 2 pressures the ball as X^4 and X^5 stand up the screeners to allow X^3 to lock and trail or go over the screens to get to 3.

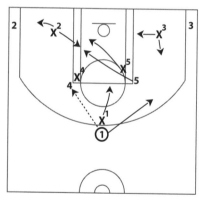

Figure 9.50
Big-to-big elbow slash in lane: X^4 pressures 4 and makes him dribble drive toward 2 and X^2. X^5 bodies up and forces 5 out above the block. X^3 guards against 5 going for the backdoor lob.

Double-Doubles. We try to lock and trail while the screener's defenders try to screen the screeners, enabling their defending teammates to lock and trail their opponents. The farther out we can stand up the screeners the better our chances of defending these multiple screens. We might switch the second screen in each double or shoot the gap. Once again, on-the-ball pressure is a must (Figure 9.49).

Elbow Pass and Dive. Each of our off-the-ball defenders must be drawn to the ball on the dribble or a pass. These defenders must be prepared to body up, beat weak-side cutters to their spots, or deny and force them high or backdoor. The player defending the ball handler at the elbow must pressure him as though the dribble was used (Figure 9.50).

Pick the Picker. We want to stand up the screeners and lock and trail or shoot the gap on the picker receiving the screen. If the weak-side corner or wing is occupied, we might switch the perimeter man on the weak side with the player defending the screener. This is a very difficult maneuver to defend when the

Figure 9.51
Pick the picker: 2 screens across for 5 as X^5 bodies up and forces 5 high. 4 then pins down for 2. X^2 shoots the gap in front of 4's screen as X^4 stands 4 up. If 2 fades, X^3 is there to help.

weak-side corner and wing have been vacated and a good screen has been set (Figure 9.51).

Pinch Post. When defending the pinch-post two-man game, the defender guarding the ball should fight over the screen on the dribble and/or go under the pinch-post player, but in front of his defensive teammate who must give space to let him through. If the screen is set high out on the floor the post defender can pinch his man and let the passer go quickly under the player with the ball, but this is dangerous unless you are sure you have weak-side help (Figure 9.52).

Pinch-Post or Low-Post Action Where the Passer Sets an Inside Screen for the Ball Carrier. This is usually a surprise move during a game and we feel the best way to handle it is to switch it aggressively and force the dribbler uphill. When we trap, our objective is to force the dribbler back to his individual defender (Figure 9.53).

Pinch Post (Pass and Follow) Two-Man Game. When defending the pinch-post two-man game on the weak side we trap the dribbler with the screener's defender, stop the ball, or force the dribbler uphill. Our other three defenders on the weak side zone up and get ready to rotate while covering the nail, elbow, and box nearest the other offensive men. They are drawn to the ball to provide the defensive help necessary to stop penetration and to shrink the floor.

If we cannot deflect or steal the pass when defending the pinch-post pass and follow, we want the post defender to step back and let the passer's defender through or we aggressively trap the ball. Stepping back and letting the defender through enables the passer's defender to beat his man to the spot and not get picked off by the screen being set as his opponent rolls to the goal or fades to position

Figure 9.52
Pinch post: we want X¹ to body up to 1 and fight over the screen as X⁴ hard shows to stop the ball. X² has the nail and X³ the weak-side elbow. X⁵ is ready to rotate big to big should 4 roll to the goal.

Figure 9.53
On the point-of-ball screen by X¹ or X⁴, we force the ball uphill, where both X¹ and X⁴ trap the receiver. X² plays the nail, and X⁵ and X³ are ready to help and rotate should 1 pop or fade.

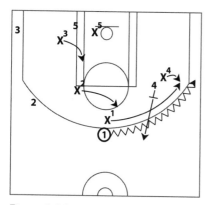

Figure 9.54
Pinch-post two-man game: X⁴ opens up
and permits X¹ to slide through in front
of him to get to 1.

Figure 9.55
Pinch-post two-man game: X⁴ opens up
and permits X¹ to slide through in front
of him to get to 1.

himself on the wing to receive the ball (Figures 9.54 and 9.55).

Flash-Post or Blind Pig Action. We want to overplay and deny the flash-post pass if possible. If we cannot and the ball is received on the post, we want the post defenders to step back, get in a wide stance, bother the passer, and get in the passing lanes. The wing's defender must keep his man in front of him if possible. If he loses his man, he either opens up, makes himself wide, and retreats to the goal, or he snaps back and tries to impede or deflect a pass to the player he is defending. The weak-side defenders must be drawn to the ball, and the nearest defender forces the initial receiver high to receive the pass. Weak-side defenders should occupy the nail, elbow, and box. *It is the responsibility of the defensive player on the low block to come across the lane to stop the offensive player trying to go backdoor* (Figures 9.56 and 9.57).

Pinch Post or Elbow Dribble Screen or Pass and Follow Action. We body up to the dribbler and fight

Figure 9.56
Flash-post or blind pig: 4 flashes to the
pinch post when recognizing the pressure and overplay of 2 by X². X⁴ must
pressure 4 as X² fights to keep 2 in
front of him. X⁵ is ready to cross the
lane and rotate, and X² must rotate and
try to get inside 5.

over the screen. We slide through in front of our defensive teammate when he passes to the post and follows his pass for a return pass. The post defender must step back and let his teammate through on a pass and follow—and also shade his man to the outside. If he can deny the first pass or force his man to receive the pass farther out on the floor, we can successfully stop the effectiveness of this maneuver (Figure 9.58).

Post Splits. When defending post splits the most important thing is that the defenders involved talk to each other. They must get level with the offensive post man with the ball to combat quick slips and cuts. They must also get level with the ball if they want to switch the players they are defending. For a defensive switch to be effective we cannot allow the cutters to split the switch and cause defensive indecision. When defending high splits or splits of any kind that may require switching, the back man is responsible for calling out both the pick and the switch. He has the best view of what the offense is trying to do (Figure 9.59).

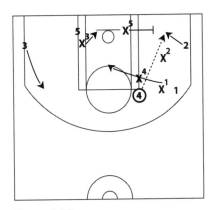

Figure 9.57
Flash-post or blind pig: X^5 crosses lane and X^2 opens up or snaps back to play 2.

Figure 9.58
Pinch-post or elbow dribble screen: this forces the pinch-post player out on the floor above the 3-point line by overplaying the pass to 4.

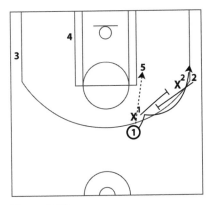

Figure 9.59
Post splits: on the pass to 5 from 1, 2 sets a back pick on X^1 as 1 cuts over the top of the screen. X^1 and X^2 come together to stop the split and aggressively switch this maneuver.

Figure 9.60
One-four flat set: X¹ wants to keep I in front of him and force to the sideline to stop penetration. We want X³ to fake and recover to the shooter on the strong side.

Defending the One-Four Flat Set. We want to keep the player with the ball in front of us or influence him toward his weak hand. Our two defenders guarding the offensive players in the corner are up in helping positions near the elbows and our two defenders guarding the low-post players are on the inside and one or two steps above the players they are guarding. We must stop penetration and not put ourselves in jeopardy by permitting the offense draw and kick opportunities. If the offense clears a man out and overloads a side, we want to tilt and cover both elbows and boxes with the four defenders not guarding the player with the ball (Figures 9.60 and 9.61).

Figure 9.61
One-four flat set: again we want to stop penetration by I and force sideline. 4 clears out and comes high, X² plays the weak-side elbow, X³ fakes and stays with 3, and X⁴ tilts to stop penetration.

10

Trapping and Double-Teaming

Trapping and double-teaming are disruptive tactics we use to surprise, confuse, unnerve, and distract our opponents. We want to get deflections and steals, which take the opposition out of their set offense and comfort zones.

Trapping

We feel it's important to teach our players to come at a right angle on our two-man, half-court trapping defense. We attack the dribbler from the blind side rather than from behind, once he crosses the half-court area near the sideline. If at all possible we don't permit the man with the ball to throw a penetrating pass out of the double-team or trap. We want our interceptors or anticipators to be in position to steal a pass made to a perimeter player or to a player in the near or far corners. We accomplish this by forcing the trapped man to pass over the trapper's outside shoulders prohibiting the penetrating or gut pass to an offensive player in the middle of the court.

We teach our interceptors to learn to read the eyes of the player being trapped. This helps them decide whether to contain the player they are guarding or go for the steal. We want to force the player being trapped to pass outside instead of to the middle or high-post area, and we must front the offensive team's post players to eliminate the most dangerous outlet pass.

Our players know the trappers in this defensive set are the two men pressuring the ball. Our next two players nearest these two defenders know they are interceptors because they have two trappers in front of them; the player farthest from the ball is the high or low goaltender because he has two interceptors as well as two trappers in front of him. Each of our off-the-ball defenders tries to read the eyes of the player being trapped to help anticipate where the next pass is likely to go.

Our objective when we trap the low post is to stop inside post domination. Our post traps are also designed to create opportunities for our perimeter defenders to force turnovers, get deflections, and make steals.

These are some situations where we might trap the low post:

1. When outstanding players post up and receive the ball on the low block
2. When an offensive post player isolates our defender and takes him on the dribble down to the low block
3. On isolation plays where we double-team the ball if we are getting hurt
4. On pick-and-roll plays to stop penetration and limit the pass inside to the screener rolling to the basket

We front the low post and keep the ball from going inside so we can stay home to pressure shooters who have open looks on the perimeter. We trap and are prepared to rotate whenever the ball is passed inside to a low-post threat.

Some teams might designate which player they send to trap by calling out that player's name from the bench, while others predetermine the trapper or trap from particular areas on the court. Coaches must decide when and how or if they want to trap or double the low post.

When digging or helping from the top or the side, the defensive man should spread himself out wide, step in, and give a full-bodied show rather than reaching in with his arm. The helping defender should step in front of dribblers and drivers to force them to commit offensive fouls, stop, and/or change direction. This defender always tries to be in a position to help and recover when guarding a player without the basketball. The player guarding the ball must apply pressure and work to keep his opponent from penetrating. If the offensive player's dribble has

Figure 10.1
Baseline drive: 2 drives toward the basket and X⁵ crosses the lane to trap the baseline drive with X². X⁴ drops back to get inside of 5, and X¹ rotates back to help check 4 and 1.

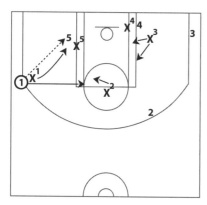

Figure 10.2
Trapping from the wing: on the pass to 5, X¹ releases with his butt to the baseline to get level with the ball. We decide to have him trap 5 immediately or to wait for one dribble. If 1 cuts middle on the trap, X² stops his cut. The trapper (X¹) turns 5 back to his defender.

been used, the defender's hands should be up and active to make passing the ball difficult. The defender should not permit forwards and centers to drive and penetrate or to make easy or uncontested passes.

In situations when we trap and the ball is passed out of the trap, we want the trapper to sprint out of the trap and be the runner. We want him to look to rotate to the free man in the direction of the pass or to be ready to help should the nearest offensive player be covered.

Your defensive schemes should include signals for trapping the first wing or perimeter pass that the offense makes, doubling the dribbler, running and jumping the dribbler, and feinting or faking traps. You should decide whether to double the post on the pass and with which defender, to double on the first or second dribble, or to aggressively front the post. If at all possible, we try to trap offensive players in the corners of the court.

Whenever we help and trap we emphasize the importance of the help never getting beat. We cannot let the offense split the trap or double-team, complete a penetrating or gut pass, or have the player with the basketball dribble through the middle of the trap.

We work on trapping and rotating in our four-against-four shell defense drill. We have the wing player with the ball drive sideline and beat his man on the baseline. We then have our weak-side low defender cross the lane, rotate, and trap while our weak-side high defender rotates back to the weak-side block. All three off-the-ball defenders are drawn toward the ball in help positions to help and shrink the floor (Figure 10.1).

Some teams front or trap the post by setting up a four-on-four half-court shell drill to demonstrate trapping from the top and trapping from the wing. In each of these instances our coaches demonstrate the weak-side help and rotation to our players before practicing our traps and rotations (Figure 10.2).

Many coaches use the tactic of fronting the low post, and some decide to play behind or three-quarter the post and have trappers coming on the pass, digging on post-ups, or doubling the post player on the dribble. We at times prefer to double or trap the post once the pass to the post is made and the passer executes a baseline cut. The defender guarding the cutter then can snap back and double the post once the passer cuts to the middle. We teach the cutter's defender to first take the cutter to the rim and then double back and trap the post. Weak-side defenders and trappers must read the eyes of the man being trapped to aid rotations and see where help is needed. It is extremely important to teach the trappers to seal the trap and always force the pass out of the trap over the defender's outside shoulder to help eliminate the penetrating or gut pass to help our interceptors steal and/or deflect the ball. We feel this denies the opposition easy scoring opportunities.

We double-team the ball in the following ways in our man-to-man defenses:

1. We double-team the first wing pass in the offensive end with the nearest defender.

Figure 10.3

Trapping from the top: on the pass to 5, X^2 seals and traps from the top of key. X^1 drops between 1 and 5 to help. X^3 is ready to cover the pass to 3 in the weak-side corner or 2 at the top. X^2 reads X^3 and rotates accordingly. X^1 rotates to 2 in this diagram and X^2 would rotate to the next free wall.

Figure 10.4

X^1 takes the baseline cutter to the rim and snaps back to trap 5 and turn him back to X^5. Our three other defenders rotate counterclockwise to help cover the backboard.

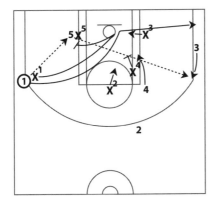

Figure 10.5

X^1 takes 1 to the rim to prevent a pass from 5 to 1 for a score. Then 1 snaps back to trap 5 with X^5. Since X^3 is occupied by 1 on the pass from 5 to 3, X^2 rotates to 3.

Figure 10.6
Doubling the first wing pass: X¹ drops line of ball and then traps 3 with X³ as X² and X⁴ look to defend the cutter and nearest outlets.

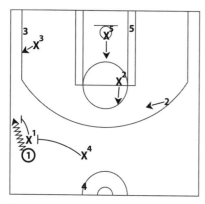

Figure 10.7
X⁴ traps the ball off of the nearest trailing offense player 4. X¹ forces 1 sideline and then X⁴ gets level with the ball to trap and blindside 1. X¹ and X⁴ are trappers, X² and X³ are interceptors, and X⁵ is the deep goaltender.

This is usually the player guarding the player that passed the ball.

2. The closest trailing defender gets level with the ball and traps the dribbler right near the mid-court area once the defender forces the dribbler sideline. This is an example of our half-court trap.

3. The trailing defender nearest the ball traps the dribbler near the sideline in the backcourt once the dribbler's back is turned. This defense is an example of a three-quarter court trap.

4. Full-court trapping including our big men. All of our other defenders are pressuring up in extended full-court shell defense.

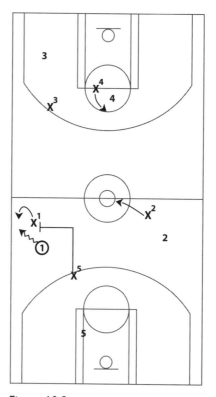

Figure 10.8
Trail defender X⁵ traps 1 from behind with X¹. X³ overplays near sideline pass, X⁴ (the goaltender) is ready to deny the gut pass, and X² gets level with the ball to stop a pass to the middle to 4 or an outlet pass to 2.

We prefer to pick up full court and trap our opponents after made field goals, made free throws, or dead-ball situations. Following misses and in transition, if our opponents push the ball, we feel it is more beneficial to pick them up early and, if possible, to contain them until we can organize, level back, and put pressure on them in the half-court. There is no point in doubling teams in transition after a miss and placing our defense in jeopardy as we attempt to match up unless our defenders are all below the ball and ready to defend.

We can also employ our run-and-jump defensive philosophy in these full-, three-quarter, and half-court defenses. A defender who is either in front of or alongside the dribbler leaves his man to run at the dribbler to either trap him or force him to pass the ball. This is a surprise tactic that often rattles the dribbler, especially if he is dribbling with his head down. Again we want to force the pass out over the trapper's outside shoulder so that our interceptors can play the passing lanes looking to steal the ball.

In our double-teaming pressure defense we again always call the two players on the ball our trappers; the next two players who are cutting off the passing lanes, anticipating, and looking to steal the ball are

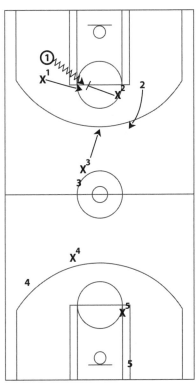

Figure 10.9
Full-court pressure: defense forcing the dribbler to the middle to trap and read the passing lanes.

Figure 10.11
Nail or plug, elbow, and box: these are the areas we refer to when providing weak-side help. We need to fill these off of the ball spots.

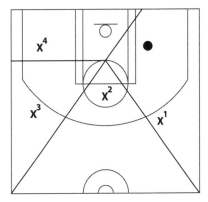

Figure 10.10
Half-court trapping areas.

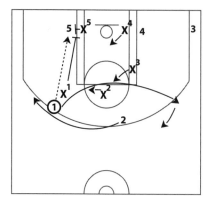

Figure 10.12
Trapping the drop from the top: players must seal, lock their inside legs, and come together when trapping.

Figure 10.13
Drop rotation: if X¹ can rotate quickly with the ball in the air, he may be able to rotate to 3 in the corner so X⁴ can stay home and front the low post.

our interceptors; and the player guarding the basket to prevent layups and easy baskets is our high or low goaltender. Many teams use their own terminology to designate these defensive positions.

Double-Teaming and Defending the Low Post

Figures 10.10 through 10.15 illustrate several ways to double-team the low post.

Trap from the Strong Side High. As shown in Figure 10.12, X^2 is our trapper from the strong-side high area. X^1 is responsible for reading the trap and denying the pass back to player 1. Our tactic is to encourage 5 to throw a lob or skip pass to the weak side. X^2 and X^5 trap post player 5. Our rotating players are responsible for covering the basket and the free-throw lane (nail) area. X^3 and X^4 are in tandem inside the weak-side elbow and box.

Rotation on Pass Out of the Post. On the pass from the post out to the top of the key, X^3 covers the pass to 2. X^4 rotates out to the weak-side wing area to take 3 and force him baseline. X^2, our original trapper, must rotate and front 4 as X^5, X^3, and X^1 rotate to the nail, weak-side elbow, and box (Figure 10.13).

Figure 10.14
Trapping the post from the strong side low. X¹ snaps back along the baseline.

Rotation When Ball Is Reversed and Player 4 Dives. When the trap is set by X² and X⁵ and player 4—spaced out at the top of the key—dives to the goal, X³ is responsible for forcing 4 behind him to pass him off to X⁴. When 5 passes to 2 at the top, X³ rotates out to 2. X⁴ then rotates out to 3 as the ball is reversed and X² rotates out of the trap and across the lane to front 4. At times we may invert X³ and X⁴ to keep our taller defender and better rebounder closest to the goal (Figures 10.16 and 10.17).

Rotation When Post Feeder Cuts. The rotation changes when the trap comes from the post feeder's defender after his opponent has cut away to the weak side and X¹ has doubled back from the front of the rim to trap 5. X², X³, and X⁴ stay home with the players they are guarding. When the ball is reversed to 1 in the opposite corner X¹ sprints out of the trap over X⁴ to recover to 1 (Figure 10.18).

Prior to each game we decide which tactic we will use based on the opponent's personnel and style of play. Here are some examples of where the trap may come:

1. Off of the passer, either when he cuts or when he spots up
2. From the nearest off-the-ball defender
3. Off of the cutter following the post entry pass by snapping back once the cutter has reached the goal
4. From a predesignated nonscorer
5. From the nearest baseline big man
6. From the weak-side high
7. When we front the post and have the weak-side big man cross the lane to play behind and sandwich the post player if he receives a lob pass
8. From centerfield (nail) or the top of the key area

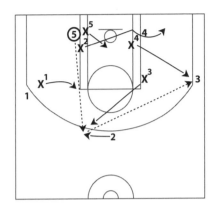

Figure 10.15
Rotation on pass out of post.

Figure 10.16
X² traps the post and the rotation when the ball is reversed and player 4 dives. X⁴ or X³ must pick up the dive man.

Figure 10.17
Rotation on wing drive.

Figure 10.18
Rotation when post feeder cuts.

Double-teams can cause players to make mistakes and turn the ball over. Here, the Seattle Supersonics attempt to double-team rising star Jamal Crawford then of the Chicago Bulls.
Photo courtesy of NBA Entertainment.

9. On the post catch with a predetermined player or from a specific area on the floor
10. Once the post player dribbles the ball (we attack from a predetermined area)
11. Not until the post player proves he warrants a double-team

We will also trap a post player if we feel he is tentative or cannot pass out of a double-team. We want to pressure him and force a turnover.

When guarding against a drop to the low post or a lob, instead of fronting the post player or three-quartering him, we will body up and play a half a man to prevent the seal and lock and lob.

Whenever we trap or double the post, our trappers must seal the inside to take away the penetrating pass and turn the offensive post player back to his defender to stop ball reversal. Our anticipators or interceptors are then in position to steal any errant pass.

Here is a post defense principle to remember: When your post defender pushes his man off of the low block, forces him to throw the ball out, and then tries to improve his position and repost, our rule requires our defender to get around the offensive player and front him to deny him open low-post position closer to the basket.

We also trap isolation plays and force the offensive player to our help. We might double on the pass or on the dribble. We mix up our traps to disrupt offensive rhythm.

The interceptor doesn't immediately come forward on a trap. He anticipates, judges how far he is from the ball and his opponent, and waits until the ball is in the air before making his move. He goes for the steal if he is 90 percent certain he can get the ball. If not, he is taught to feint the trap or steal.

When we trap the ball we leave the offensive man farthest from the ball free. We encourage the long skip pass across the court to that player. We use this tactic when the offensive post player with the ball turns his back to the defense and our next nearest defender goes and traps; in other words, we then treat this situation as a baseline drive.

The term *buddy system* is explained when it comes to teaching players how to provide strong- and weak-side help for the defender on the ball. Our defender's buddies are the two nearest teammates on his immediate left and right. They are responsible for working with him in any trap or double-teaming situation. When we trap, we always want two trappers, two interceptors, and a high or low goaltender. Our alignment almost always looks like a two-two-one zone defense when two of our players are trapping the ball, as shown in Figure 10.19.

Here are some of the guidelines we follow in our pressing or pressure zone defenses:

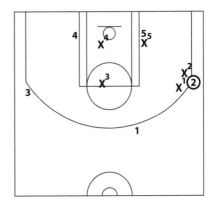

Figure 10.19

Two-two-one zone trap: X¹ and X² are trappers. X⁵ and X³ are interceptors. X⁴ is the deep goaltender. Buddies are the teammates to each defensive player's immediate left and right.

1. Whichever defense we use we want to shade the ball and shadow or match up with the offensive player in the immediate area we are defending. We always want to play the ball tough by pressuring the player with the ball.

2. We have three pressure defensive rules we absolutely must follow:

    ★ The ball cannot be passed to the middle of the floor. No gut passes!

    ★ We cannot permit an offensive player to split us with the dribble. We seal all traps!

    ★ We cannot permit an offensive player with the ball to beat us on the sideline or the baseline (the short side of the court). We force sideline and baseline and stop the ball and treat it as if it were a baseline drive.

3. We trap as aggressively as the situation warrants. We have to be prepared to mix up our coverage by using both slow and quick traps as well as faking or feinting traps. The trapper must always quickly sprint out of the

trap once the ball has been passed. He must move on the pass, not on the catch.

4. We designate the corners of the court as our trapping areas as well as the areas on either side of the mid-court line. When the ball is above the free-throw line, the trap involves the two nearest players at a right angle to the ball—normally a guard and a wing. When the ball is below the foul line the trap should involve the wing and baseline player nearest the ball.

5. If possible, we want our two trappers to have the legs nearest each other crossed to help prevent the trap from being split by the offensive player with the ball.

6. We trap aggressively with hands up to trace, deflect, or steal the ball. We also try to force the man with the ball back to our other trapping defender and bump the offensive player with our chests and not with our hands. We believe that deflections lead to steals and easy baskets.

7. We shut down all penetrating or gut passes. We force passes uphill away from the corners or across the top and in front of us. We place a special emphasis on not fouling and losing our advantage when we trap.

8. Whenever an offensive player is passing, dribbling, or shooting, we put pressure on the ball.

9. Defenders must communicate and alert teammates when offensive players duck into the lane or flash up to the high post from the weak side.

10. We rebound defensively with all five of our players. We don't want our opponents to rebound offensively and get second shots that lead to easy baskets.

11. Once a ball is passed out of a corner trap we want to match up and recover back to

our man or area as quickly as possible. On skip passes we must rotate and scramble back to a free man in the direction of the help or pass to get level with the ball.

In each of our one-guard-front pressure defenses the defensive point man must pick up early and channel or influence the ball to one side or the other to enable us to trap in the corners or at mid-court. The pressure defender, when he is not involved in a corner trap, is responsible for retreating or dropping back to the middle to deter post entries. He must learn to read the eyes of the player being trapped and be ready to anticipate and steal the pass out of the double team.

The wing nearest the ball in our press must be ready to trap once the ball is passed into his area. The weak-side wing then must control the middle of the floor to deny the gut or penetrating pass. Both the wings and the point man must work together as if attached by a string. The weak-side wing cannot release or vacate the middle of the floor until he allows the strong-side wing to recover and replace him. We try not to initiate our trap until we pressure and force the offensive player with the ball to put it on the floor. Again, we do not want to permit the dribbler to penetrate the middle or to beat us with the dribble on the short side of the floor.

If the fronted offensive player in the mid-post area drops to the baseline, the wing man fronting him drops to the low-post area and continues to front. The opposite defensive big man helps on the weak side to prevent lob passes and must be in position to rebound the ball.

We use our one-and-done principle when we trap in the corner, usually on a skipped pass across court to the weak side. The trapping defender sprints out of the trap and looks to pick up a free man in the middle or on the perimeter. We sprint, match up, and are automatically in a man-to-man defense whenever a skip pass is made out of the corner. We must control the middle of the court and keep the offense and the ball out on the perimeter. If the pass from the corner is made out to the top of the key, the trapper sprints out of the trap to close out and recover. He must make sure to take away any dribble penetration to the middle of the floor. Keeping the ball on the perimeter is our goal and we must close out on all shooters with a hand up, under control. We do not want to run by the shooter and provide the offense with draw-and-kick opportunities. We close out short on drivers and long on shooters.

The defensive player covering the baseline must protect the goal and guard anyone in his area. He cannot vacate the basket area until a teammate rotates back to cover the goal. If his man moves to the corner he must communicate with the wing on that side and get him to shadow the area until he can safely get there.

The baseline defender is able to challenge a pass over the wing's head, especially if he knows that he will be receiving weak-side help. On a pass to the corner the weak-side wing covers back or the baseline defender rotates out with everyone else matching up with an offensive player. It is imperative that rotating defenders sprint to take the free men in the direction of the help. We never gamble or close out aggressively on players we know are not strong offensive threats. We are much more apt to help and recover in these instances unless we are 90 percent certain that we can get a steal. At times we can match up and play our opponent's baseline rover, man-to-man as he cuts along the baseline from the weak side to the strong side of the court by sending our weak-side defender with him while keeping our taller defenders at home to protect the goal to defend offensive low-block players. Our back or baseline defenders are our high or low goaltenders and they are responsible for alerting teammates in front of them of players flashing to the high post to attack the defense from behind.

Trapping Drill

A coach passes the ball to a player and two defenders guard the ball handler in the backcourt. The defenders try to contain and/or trap the dribbler for 8 or 10 seconds in the backcourt. We also run this drill in the front court by passing the ball to the offensive player near a corner as the two defenders try to trap and contain the offensive player without allowing him to split them or beat them on either side of the court (Figure 10.20).

Figure 10.20
Half-court trap: this is two defenders versus one ball handler. Coach passes to 3 and defenders X⁴ and X¹ try to trap and contain him without fouling. We also do this in backcourt and contain for 8 to 10 seconds.

11

Transition Defense and Drills

It is my feeling that outstanding transition defense is the trademark of a great defensive team. If you are able to stop your opponents from getting quick fast-break scores and easy early offense baskets, you will severely limit their offensive production. You must also have defensive floor balance if you expect to win basketball games.

Transition Defense

One way to teach fast-break and transition defense is to set up a defensive drill that begins with two against one, then progresses to three against two, then four against three, five against four, and finally

It is important to contest every shot—no matter what. Here, the effort of All-Star Elton Brand of the Los Angeles Clippers thwarts a would-be dunk by Sacramento's Keon Clark.
Photo courtesy of NBA Entertainment.

five against five. This is a continuous drill; it doesn't stop until we complete all five sequences.

We try not to foul our opponents needlessly. That said, we don't permit easy layups or uncontested shots. Part of our strategy is that we commit hard fouls that will prevent three-point plays. We force the opposition to make two free throws. Team steals are also important but not when we try to get them in transition by trying to steal the ball in the backcourt. This will leave our team further outnumbered and vulnerable in transition.

Knowing when your teammates are liable to shoot will aid your defensive transition. We believe in devoting 40 to 60 percent of our practice time to defense and rebounding. Most coaches stress having their players rebound offensively, which is why we always rebound *defensively* with five players instead of having our perimeter players leak out early. We don't want to give up second-chance baskets.

Suggested Transition Defense Drills

1. Full-court five-against-five set with players matched up against each other
2. Four defenders against five offensive players with a defensive trailer added once the basketball crosses half-court
3. Five-against-five set after rebounding a missed shot, causing a deflection or turnover
4. Fast breaking off of a free throw following either a make or a miss

Steps to Emphasize When Teaching Great Transition Defense

1. The first defender back must retreat to the paint, cover the goal, and build the defense out. The first big man back in transition must pick up the first inside offensive player back—not necessarily his own individual opponent.

2. All other defenders must try to get level or below the line of the ball.

3. It is imperative that we always contain and pressure the dribbler and stop the ball.

4. Each retreating defender must quickly match up with a player near the goal even though it is not necessarily his particular opponent and verbally communicate this switch to his retreating teammates.

5. Everyone must help to stop penetration by a full-bodied show or faking and feinting at the player with the basketball.

6. We must always establish both weak-side and ball-side help.

7. All five defenders must contest shots and block out.

8. Players must not flail at or aimlessly try to steal the ball in the backcourt on transition defense. To do so places retreating teammates in very difficult positions.

Tip: It is much more difficult for players to stop the ball and pick up their men in transition if the opponent is playing a zone defense and wishes to run. That's because in such cases players will very rarely be matched up against their own individual opponents. It is very important that your players try to level back to the line of the ball to stop the opposition's fast break.

If we cannot match up, we must sprint back, pack the paint, and build our defense out from in front of the goal.

Four-Against-Four and Five-Against-Five Defensive Transition Drill

A team that quickly changes from offense to defense, stops the ball, and doesn't permit layups and easy baskets will very likely control the tempo of the game. Another characteristic of great transition-defense teams is that they rebound offensively with two and a half players to ensure proper defensive balance. Rebounding aggressively on offense will stop the opposition from running out for easy high-percentage baskets because they have to concentrate on boxing out rebounders to prevent giving up second-chance points.

In transition when the opponent's big men run out to the front of the rim it is the responsibility of the first big man back to corral the first offensive big man down the floor regardless of whether or not that

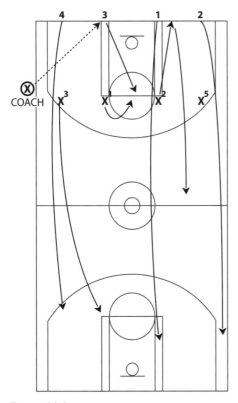

Figure 11.1
Players are lined up facing each other but not necessarily matched up to their own individual opponents. Coach has the ball, passes to a player, and calls a defensive player's number (2). That defender must run and touch the baseline. The four offensive players run a fast break and big to big match up, protect the goal, and stop the ball until X^2 has recovered and picked up the free offensive player.

is his specific defensive assignment. Big men must work together on defense as well as offense. They must be made aware of the importance of helping and supporting one another at all times.

It is imperative in transition defense that the first defender back covers the goal. Once that is accomplished the next most important tasks are to talk, stop, and contain the ball. This will enable the other defenders to level back and pick up their opponents. Teach your players that if the man they are guarding has been picked up in transition, they must then pick up the next free man closest to the basket. Don't allow a player to run back to his assigned man who is now covered and leave another man free. Emphasize that if they must leave a man free as they hustle back on defense, it should be the man farthest from the ball and the basket on the perimeter. It is the responsibility of every one of your players to get at least *level* with the ball in transition. After the first pass is made, while his teammates are in a tandem defense setup, the third man back on defense should go to the weak-side area of the court to set up a defensive triangle.

Defensive Fast-Break Drills

Continuous Two Against One, Three Against Two, Four Against Three, Five Against Four, and Five Against Five. This drill provides an opportunity to practice transition defense in various situations. Divide your squad into groups of five. Use the full court. Your players must stop the ball, protect the goal, and pick up their men. This drill fosters communication and recognition. Emphasize talking on defense.

Remind players that they must be aware of opponents leaking out when their team shoots jump shots or their point guard penetrates. You must constantly preach defensive balance if you want to be a great defensive team. The nearest teammate on the perimeter is responsible for stopping the penetrators.

Three-Against-Two Full-Court Defensive Transition Drill. This and many other progressive fast-break drills are described in Chapter 15.

Four-Against-Four Full-Court Transition Drill. Set up two equal lines of four players. The defensive players are on the foul line facing the baseline and the offensive players are on the baseline facing the opposite basket. A coach passes the ball to an offensive player, and the defensive player in front of him must run to touch the foul line and then run back in defensive transition to try to catch the other seven players who are attempting a four-versus-three fast break. The defense must get back in transition, match up, stop the ball, and protect the goal. The trailing defender has to sprint to get level with the ball and pick up the free offensive player who is probably not his original opponent. The transition is not complete until the offensive group scores or the defensive team recovers or rebounds the ball.

Five-Against-Five Full-Court Transition Drill. This is the same as the previous drill, but if the offense scores they must quickly make the change from offense to defense and the defense makes the change from defense to offense. We always try to run a play after made shots and we look to fast break or run our secondary or early offense following misses or steals.

Fast Break Following a Made or Missed Free Throw. In this drill we set up our defense before we shoot a free throw and then try to stop the offensive team as they run for a score. Many teams will try to run and score after a make as well as a miss, and we must be prepared to defend this tactic. This drill also provides us with an opportunity to practice our full- and half-court pressure and pressing defenses against many different offensive free-throw line alignments.

12

Zone, Press, and Combination Defenses

We constantly practice changing defenses after time-outs, dead balls, end of quarters or halves, and free throws in order to keep our opponents off balance and to change the tempo of the game.

Full-Court Defenses

We begin to build our full-court press defense by going one against one full court, two against two full court, three against three full court, and four against four full court before demonstrating our full-court man-to-man press to our team. We emphasize positioning in each of our full-court shell sequences to the point of even showing our players how we want them to position themselves to best see the ball and their opponent. We like players off of the ball to be positioned so that they have the foot and hand nearest the ball forward. This helps them with their peripheral vision and enables them to see more of the court and passing lanes. We place a great deal of importance on our players knowing where their help comes from and where we are trying to force, influence, or channel the ball. We want to take away our opponent's ability to throw the wide outlet pass from the middle of the court. We work on our run-and-jump defense, forcing the dribbler to turn his back so the next nearest defender can double him from his blind side as well as perfecting our weak-side rotations.

As a coach you must make a decision as to whether to trap once in a one-and-done situation (to possibly steal the ball or slow the offense), or whether to trap every time an opportunity presents itself. It's imperative that each of your players understands your philosophy and the defensive concept of leveling with the ball and not trailing the play when his individual opponent is trailing behind the ball. The leveling defender is in a great position to double-team the ball from a trailing position, as well as in a position to deflect the dribble from behind as he sprints back in transition. Again, in defensive transition, the first man back covers the goal, and the next man back must locate and stop or control the basketball. You must decide which press defense you should employ and should consider whether you prefer to have your big man play and pressure the ball out of bounds or to shadow the opposing team's point guard, making it difficult for the guard to receive the ball and initiate the offense. Some coaches prefer to shadow press early to try to keep their opponents from establishing an early rhythm and flow to their offense.

Full-Court Press Defensive Philosophy

When discussing pressure defenses some coaches differentiate between the run-and-jump and the run-and-trap or double-team. Some prefer to run and jump on the perimeter and run and trap or double-team on the baseline. Using the run-and-jump on the perimeter can help get the ball out of the opposing point guard's hands. You usually run and jump when the nearest defender to the dribbler being pressured doesn't have too far to go to effectively help get the ball out of the ball handler's hands. You also run and jump when you don't want to give the offense time to make good decisions. This defensive tactic forces them to make hurried and spontaneous decisions. Many times in the guts of the game we want to change the tempo by surprising our opponents with a different form of defensive pressure.

Not many NBA teams pressure and pick up the point guard early. Some say playing 82 games a season will wear out your point guard and perimeter players because it is difficult to get your other players to push up, overplay, and pressure the opponent's pressure releases at the same time. We believe anything is possible but it is determined by the ability and work ethic of your players. We also always want to have the element of surprise as a factor in our favor.

UCLA coach John Wooden used to have his team zone press full or three-quarter court and then fall back into a man-to-man to confuse the opponent. Some coaches feel that you should fall back into the same type of defense as your press. Other coaches will experiment with man-to-man full-court pressure and then fall back into a zone with the emphasis on each man getting to a predetermined spot in a defensive zone alignment based on who can fill the spot first. Size is of secondary importance because they are not using this defense for every possession. Pressing and doubling is most effective when the defenders constantly fake and feint the trap to keep the offense off balance.

Some coaches believe in playing a zone when their team has the lead in the fourth quarter. They want to take away the opposition's easy-opportunity baskets, shorten the number of possessions in the game, and try to stay out of foul trouble.

On the other hand, other coaches feel their team has difficulty getting back to their own men in transition when the opposition plays a zone; that's because many teams playing a zone want to beat the other team down court before it has a chance to set up its defense. We have experimented with playing a full-court press with three perimeter defenders playing man-to-man and the two tallest men zoning up down the floor and then having all five defenders fall back and play a two-three zone. Sometimes we even use a man-to-man defense once the ball has crossed the mid-court line. Changing your full-court pressure defenses can enable you to cover the defensive goal and disrupt offensive flow.

Playing a zone takes time off of the shot clock. Many times the offense struggles to recognize what kind of defense you are playing. Some coaches believe in playing a two-two-one or one-two-one-one zone press before dropping back into different zones to confuse and baffle opponents. Other coaches might play man-to-man, trap with a rover or designated trapper once the ball is passed into the front court, and zone up or play a combination of man-to-man and zone defense. The defense you employ depends on your personnel and the abilities of your team to adjust to different situations.

Team Defense Calls and Signals

Teams normally have a numbering system to designate the types of defenses they use. The following is one example:

10—Combination or gimmick defenses to take a team out of their set offense

20—Normal man-to-man or basic defense

30—Run-and-jump or run-and-switching defense with the ball in front of you

40—Trapping and double-teaming defense from behind the ball

50—Zone defenses

Coaches using the above numbering system will have the last digit of their defensive calls determine where they want to initiate their defensive pressure. For example:

4—Full-court pressure

3—Three-quarter court pressure

2—Half-court pressure

1—Perimeter pressure

No matter which numbering system, signal, or designation you use, make it simple and easy for your players to remember.

Teams may also have key terms to describe the type of defensive pressure they want to put on the ball. They might use the word *hard* when they want to really pressure the player taking the ball out of bounds, and *soft* if they want his defender to drop back into the passing lanes to look to trap or steal the first pass. They might use the term *marry* or *deny* to stop the opposing point guard or best ball handler from getting the ball back once he has passed it to a teammate.

One of my closest coaching confidants when I was the head men's basketball coach at Stony Brook State University and C. W. Post College on Long Island was Ed Krinsky of Long Island's Westbury High School. Krinsky, who is now the director of the USBL (United States Basketball League) and still one of my closest basketball sounding boards, used a system that was extremely effective for his teams, one we both feel strongly can be implemented today at every level of the game. Over the years we have had many discussions concerning the value of changing defenses. We both believe that once you have established a sound fundamental man-to-man defensive philosophy with your team, innovation is the key to great defense.

We believe that an aggressive pressure defense is the most effective way to trigger your offense and generate easy baskets. Our next premise is that the key to attacking any defense starts with recognizing what type of defense your opponents are playing. Whenever you can disguise your defense you delay the offensive recognition of your tactics and give your team an advantage. To keep our opponents off balance we try to employ several defenses during the course of a game. However, we do not get into changing team defense concepts until we have prepared our players individually in terms of their proper defensive stance, footwork, use of hands, and so on. In our early practices we believe in teaching strong basic fundamental man-to-man principles; we stress controlling and defending the opposition by setting up competitive one-against-one individual drills. We then progress to two-against-two and three-against-three drills that introduce our run-and-jump tactics. In these drills we teach our players to run and trap whenever they feel they have an advantage. They learn to fake the trap if they cannot get to the dribbler in time to cause him to pick up his dribble or pass the ball. If we do trap and the ball is passed, our players sprint out of the trap and rotate to where the help came from. We teach and remind our players that they should always take the free man

Chauncey Billups typifies the aggressive style of defense the Detroit Pistons preach. Here Chauncey is pictured fighting through the screen of Samaki Walker to steal the ball from Laker superstar Kobe Bryant.

Photo courtesy of NBA Entertainment.

in the direction of the help if the player they were originally guarding is covered.

Krinsky's run-and-jump full-court press was called the Carolina defense; it was based in part on some mimeographed notes that he had gotten from Coach Smith of North Carolina more than 40 years ago. He explains, in an interesting aside, that almost all of his own coaching notes, books, and clinic and practice outlines were "borrowed" by a young coach who promised to make copies and return them. That was seven years ago and he is still waiting. We all know that coaches are great imitators as well as innovators and much of what they teach and use has been culled from other sources and coaches. Coaches are no different than comedians in this regard—they borrow from and imitate one another. However, you must return what you borrow.

Pressure Defenses

The following are some of the pressure defenses that our teams have employed. Note that the defense chosen depends upon which player scores. Many coaches key their defenses after a field goal, a made free throw, or when and where the first pass is made, but, in my experience, not many teams decide on which defense to use depending on who scores.

Diamond Zone Press. This is a one-two-one-one full-court zone defense. Pressure is put on the inbounds passer by the tallest defensive player following a made free throw. This defender tries to get a piece of the ball whenever possible, often batting it out of bounds. Whenever he is able to accomplish this it takes away the inbounds passer's ability to run the baseline to enter the basketball on the next pass, which enables the defender to now really apply pressure on the passer. The next objective is to cut off the pass to the middle by anyone trying to break pressure by posting up—and to cut off the pass to the side of the court away from the ball. The objective is to channel the pass to the nearest sideline. Once this pass is made the receiver starts his dribble down the sideline. It is then the wing defensive player's job to get to a spot on the sideline and force the dribbler to stop or change direction. The player who defended the inbounds passer follows the pass and traps the dribbler once he is stopped along the sideline. It is then up to the coach to make some adjustments in the movements of the players in accordance with their individual defensive strengths and weaknesses.

This full-court diamond press is based on John Wooden's one-two-one-one full-court zone press at UCLA. Krinsky's and my teams both used the diamond press whenever our center scored, whether from the field or the free-throw line.

North Carolina Press. Krinsky's North Carolina press incorporated man-to-man pressure with run-and-jump defensive tactics. His players constantly worked on forcing the dribbler into a trap. If the trap was avoided and the ball was passed, the player who was guarding the dribbler then rotated in the direction of where the trapper came from. It was his responsibility to pick up the free man in the direction of the help. Krinsky used this variation of the UNC press whenever one of his forwards scored the ball, whether from the field or the free-throw line.

St. Joseph's Press. The St. Joseph's press was used when either of the guards scored, whether from the field or the free throw line. They faked a three-quarter-court man-to-man press and quickly dropped back into the front court. Once the ball crossed the mid-court line they jumped the ball and attacked from a three-one-one half-court zone trap defensive alignment. Krinsky got the basics of this defense from articles written by Dr. Jack Ramsey and by traveling to Philadelphia to watch Ramsey's great

St. Joseph's teams when Krinsky first began coaching at Westbury.

The primary job of the defender in the middle of the defense is to keep the ball from going into the high post. Sometimes they will purposely channel the ball to the corner and then trap the corner with their baseline defender and the wing nearest the ball. The middle defender at the free-throw line fronts the low post and the other two high defenders retreat and defend the free-throw line and the weak-side block (nail and elbow). We use the same tactics and rules today in our one-three-one half-court zone defense.

In our discussions Krinsky and I often talked about using additional zone press alignments; for example, running the one-two-one-one diamond zone press without pressuring the inbounds passer and using the two-two-one full-court zone press at times to change the tempo and disrupt the offensive flow of our opponents. We also discussed changing our half-court defense after every time-out regardless of which team had called the time-out and then we both were able to incorporate this tactic into our coaching philosophies.

We have used the following half-court defenses after missed shots.

1. Straight man-to-man defense
2. A defense alignment where we run and jump at every opportunity when the ball is in the backcourt
3. Two-one-two zone defense when our opponent overloads the zone to one side. We then have our best defensive forward cover the weak side. He is then instructed to go out hard on the wing and challenge the outside shot when the ball is reversed or skipped.
4. One-three-one zone defense

If we decide to zone when defending the under-the-basket out-of-bounds play, we normally set up in a tight two-three close to the basket. Then we sometimes use a very unconventional tactic by double-teaming the inbounds passer with both our center and our power forward on the ball side. The other weak-side forward has the responsibility of covering the baseline away from the ball. In effect, we try to trap the inbounds passer because we realize he can't move his feet and take a step laterally or to the side without committing a traveling violation. Our guards then drop all the way back under the basket and look to intercept a high pass or bat it down court for an easy basket. As a surprise move this tactic may cause several turnovers a game if a team's inbound passer is not very good. Again, this is an example of a tactic we use to take something away from or disrupt our opponent.

In practicing our zone defense we concentrate on our positioning depending on the location of the ball by walking the ball to different areas on the court. We then add offensive players to the equation and demonstrate how we want each player to position himself in relation to the ball and each offensive player. To reinforce the importance of proper defensive positioning on the court in relation to the ball, we find it beneficial to have our team walk through our various defenses during our practices immediately before we anticipate using the defense against a particular opponent.

Krinsky said his players loved the uniqueness of this St. Joseph's strategy and felt it gave them a psychological advantage over their opponents.

Our zone defense strategy is not used to hide a weak defensive player. Each of our players must be defensively sound so that we are able to take full advantage of his particular skills and talents.

In my coaching career we have also used various defenses during a season or during the course of a game. The basic foundation of our defense has always been to teach strong man-to-man defense along with help or support principles. Once our team can guard individual opponents one against one, we expand to two against two, three against three, four against four, and five against five on both the half- and full court. Our man-to-man defense is based on the premise that the player defending the ball knows he will always have weak-side support, help, and communication from his teammates.

Face-Guard Press. We sometimes use a full-court man-to-man face-guard press after made free throws and dead balls on the baseline. In this type of press we pressure the inbounds passer with our nearest big man, trying to influence an entry pass to one side of the court. Once the ball is entered we immediately trap the ball with our big man and closest defender. We deny the outlets nearest the ball and force the receivers up the court with body-to-body pressure. We want our opponents to attempt to throw long passes up the court, which our interceptors can then pick off or deflect. Once a pass is made the player defending the ball yells "Ball!" alerting the defenders sprinting back to get level with the ball with arms raised in the passing lanes to deflect or intercept passes. We teach and work on encouraging the players sprinting back to look over their shoulders to locate the ball as they quickly retreat down the court.

At times in our face-guard press we will not pressure the inbound passer; instead, we'll use a rover in the middle of the court to anticipate and look to steal the inbounds pass as our other four defenders body up and face guard their opponents.

We realize that we won't always steal the ball in this aggressive press and that sometimes our opponents may score against it, but we believe that if we give up one basket to get two or three, in the long run our aggressiveness will work in our favor by disrupting the offense and changing the tempo of the game. We also have special defenses for particular opponents and we try to spend time in practice working on each defense for a short period of time.

We have also used a one-two-one-one full-court zone press after made free throws with pressure either on the ball or off; a two-two-one three-quarter-court press in which we want to have the offense use up the time on the shot clock; and a one-three-one three-quarter-court press to change the game's tempo.

Each of these full- or three-quarter-court defenses serves a definite purpose, and each is based on our sound man-to-man defense support principles. We prefer to force the ball down the sideline, front the high post to eliminate the gut pass in the middle of the court, hard seal and trap the ball in the corners, eliminate penetrating passes, pressure and deny the nearest outlets when the dribble is used, and utilize run-and-jump tactics on players we think we can force to dribble with their heads down.

The rules for all of our full-court defenses incorporate and follow the rules we have established for our trapping defense. We are always basically aligned in an extended two-two-one zone defensive alignment once we trap the ball. We have two trappers on the basketball and two interceptors—one ready to anticipate and steal or force the next pass to the nearest sideline and the other ready to deny the penetrating or gut pass in the middle of the court. On a perimeter pass the player fronting the high post doesn't leave his man until his rotating teammate leaves the trap and recovers to the middle. The goaltender is our last line of defense and he defends the basket and talks to and helps his teammates by encouraging the long pass to the offensive player farthest from the goal.

Our interceptors always read the eyes of the player being trapped to try to anticipate his next pass, and our trappers try to turn the player being trapped back toward the sideline while forcing any pass over their outside shoulders and away from the basket. Once the ball has been passed out of the trap, our original trapper sprints back to cover our most vulnerable area nearest the basket.

We have previously mentioned coaches setting their full-court defense depending on which of their players scores the basket. If the center scores they play a full-court one-two-two or one-two-one-one with the man who scored pressuring the ball and the inbounds passer. If either forward scores they play a two-one-two or two-two-one full-court trapping defense, and if either guard scores they play full-court pressure man-to-man defense. This tactic might suit your team as well.

In addition to our normal half-court man-to-man defense we have also played various zones—a compact one-one-three, which is very much like a standard two-three zone; an extended and aggressive trapping one-one-three; a two-one-two standard zone in the half-court; and a one-two-two zone with our third tallest defender playing the point, always staying in line with the ball and the basket to help him front the post once the ball has been passed to a wing from the top of the key. We also play a two-one-two trapping zone on some out-of-bounds possessions when we want to channel the ball to the corner and then trap it.

In each of our zones we want to front the post, pressure the ball with one defender (unless we are trapping), stop penetration, seal the passing lanes, and show a two-two-one look once the ball is on the wing or in the corner while still adhering to all of our basic defensive principles. We also still continually emphasize not letting our opponents reverse the basketball.

A combination type defense that many teams use on the half-court is the match-up zone in which they show a zone defense alignment and, for example, once the first pass is made or a man cuts through the zone, play straight man-to-man defense. Many teams also play a diamond-and-one defense or a box-and-one defense with four men playing zone and one defender guarding and harassing the opponent's best offensive threat. This defender, playing man to man, tries to deny the offensive player the ball by shadowing him all over the court. Should he receive the ball, the closest zone defender helps double-team him. When you play these defenses, your purpose in denying the best player the ball is to dare the best player's teammates to beat you.

I personally favor using a triangle-and-two combination defense at times when I feel we can disrupt our opponent's offensive rhythm by playing a three-man triangle zone close to the basket from the foul line in, and playing man-to-man denial and pressure and shadow defense against the opposition's two best perimeter scorers if your opponent's offense is heavily dependent on their scoring abilities.

We don't normally use this defense on a consistent basis, but we have it in our bag of tricks in case we need it. We feel it is a great defensive tactic to use as a surprise in a play-off environment. Many players can beat one defender, but have trouble when they are double-teamed or shadowed. The triangle-and-two is not something that every team is prepared to play against, and using it for only a short period of time can make offenses tentative. Our strategy has the same effect as pressing and trapping and then faking the press and the trap to unsettle opponents.

We have also used a half-court three-player man-to-man defense and a two-man zone on occasion. We have even used and extended this type of combination defense by having our three perimeter players pressing full court after a made free throw or a dead ball, using run-and-jump tactics or aggressively switching with these three players while our two tallest defenders run back and cover the goal in a tandem or horizontal defensive alignment. When we employ this defense we usually fall back into a two-three, one-two-two, or two-one-two type of zone defense once the ball crosses half-court. Again, we are buying time trying to make the defense use up valuable time on the shot clock. If your players are well schooled defensively you might also fall back into a man-to-man defense once the ball has crossed the mid-court line.

Zone Defenses

Many teams in the NBA play straight zone defenses since the new rules now permit it, but they also play match-up zones and combination defenses to take advantage of the 24-second clock. They sometimes set up in a normal zone and stay in it until two passes are made in the half-court. After the second pass they go to a straight man-to-man defense staying with the player they are matched up with in the zone for the remainder of the possession.

Teams especially like to use this and other zone tactics when their opponents have the ball out on the sideline or baseline with 14 or fewer seconds on the shot clock. In the NBA when a nonshooting foul occurs with less than 14 seconds on the shot clock, the clock is immediately reset to 14 seconds, not to the lesser time that was remaining on the clock when the whistle was blown. If no foul is called and the ball goes out of bounds off of the defense the shot-clock time remains the same; if the clock shows less than 14 seconds to go on any out-of-bounds play, teams might set up in a zone defense.

We don't always zone up on out-of-bounds plays. Instead we use the threat of the zone as a disruptive tactic. We feel teams don't have a great deal of time to set up and run their zone offenses with 14 seconds or less on the clock. Consequently we might force them to make a hurried or ill-advised shot attempt.

Michael Holton's University of Portland 32 and 32T Defenses. The 32 is designed to dictate or change the tempo using three-quarter-court pressure. The 32T incorporates the same concepts with more specific (and focused) traps. The lead position in this pressure defense is the top player. This is typically your most athletic player, the one you believe can disrupt a dribbler and direct or channel the player

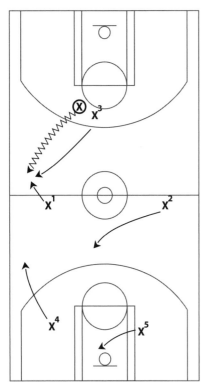

Figure 12.1
32/32T: three-quarter court trapping defense.

with the ball toward the front-line trappers (X^1 or X^2). At this point, the trap can come in the form of a hard trap or a soft show, depending on the tone that is being set. The opposite wing must drop to the middle of the floor, and the back line (X^4 and X^5) must rotate to take away the next passes. If the ball is reversed out of the trap, X^3 then follows the dribbler and directs the ball handler to another trap. The defense falls back into a three-two zone once the ball handler crosses half-court.

University of Portland 2 and 2T Half-Court Trap Defenses. The 2 is a half-court three-two zone that is designed to keep teams off balance and playing around the perimeter. The 2T is a zone that is designed to trap the first pass to the wing or corner.

Wing Trap. On the pass from 1 to 2, the top, X^1, and the wing, X^2, trap 2. The other wing, X^3, rotates to zone up the middle and does not deny the pass back to the point. The bottom player, X^5, denies the corner and the final post player, X^4 (goaltender), zones up with the weak-side wing, X^3, to defend three players.

Corner Trap. If we are trapping the corner, we trap from the wing, X^2, and the post, X^5. The opposite post defender, X^4, must front 5. Again, we must zone up away from the free man, defending two players with one.

One-One-Three Zone Half-Court Defense. This is a variation of our two-three zone defense. With the ball at the top of the key in this defense we come together and switch any cross screen to prevent the offensive players from locking and sealing to post up. By switching we create an opportunity to front the post-up to avoid getting caught in a mismatch situation.

Figure 12.2
2/2T.

Figure 12.3
Wing trap.

Figure 12.4
Corner trap.

13

Defending Special Situations

Another key to winning defensive basketball is having your team prepared to defend any situation that might occur during the course of a game. You want them confident in their knowledge that they are prepared to handle every situation and that there will be no surprises. You must pay attention to detail.

Getting Your Team Prepared

As a coach you should prepare your team to double-team, trap, full-court press, and zone. For example, you can set up two- and five-minute drills in which one team is ahead, tied, or trailing. Practice for any eventuality or situation that you think might present itself. Many games go down to the wire and the final score comes down to a difference of one or two points. Your team must always be poised and prepared to make the winning play. You must expose your players to these situations during practice. This will help them respond to pressure when they have to react instinctively and instantaneously to make the right game-winning decision. Your defense must have the confidence to get stops—whether by causing turnovers, getting steals and defensive rebounds, forcing your opponent to take a bad shot, or causing a shot-clock violation. Keep these things in mind:

1. Your players must be schooled in pressing and pressuring your opponents.
2. Your team should practice executing special defensive tactics using the full, half- and three-quarter court, as well as the baseline and the corners when your team is ahead, tied, or behind in the score.
3. Your players should be aware of the best areas to trap or double-team the ball.
4. Players must work on denying shooters or outstanding ball handlers.

5. Set up, simulate, and defend last-second shots and different score scenarios in which your team is ahead, behind, or tied.

6. Show your team how to defend a team that runs a fast break off of a free throw.

7. Prepare your players to control the ball on jump-ball situations and when they want to tip or channel the ball.

8. Make sure your players know their assignments for boxing or blocking out on all free-throw attempts.

9. Teach your players which player to foul—and when—at those times when they need to stop the clock and lengthen the game.

10. Players must fully understand that the last shot doesn't beat you in a close game, but the offensive rebound does. Don't let your players watch the ball and hope it doesn't go in while an offensive player anticipates the miss, grabs the rebound, and scores.

11. You don't want to foul when you double-team. Keep the opposition off the free-throw line.

12. During time-outs your players should be informed as to whether or not either team is in the bonus situation.

13. Make certain your players are aware of everything they need to know when they want to stop the clock and lengthen the game if your team is trailing in the game's final moments.

14. Make sure your players understand where to try to tap or throw the ball to save it from going out of bounds so your team has a chance to retrieve it.

15. There are many situations when it's crucial for a defender to take a foul to stop a fast-break basket. Are your players aware of the value of this tactic?

Special Situations

1. Think about what you might have to do in the event you have to miss a free throw and rebound when trailing in the last few seconds of a game. Is your team ready to respond effectively on their own when there are no time-outs left?

2. Does your team have hybrid or special defenses to use in certain situations?

3. If your opponents make a run and score two or three quick baskets, do your players understand the importance of getting an immediate defensive stop? Many times this is a collective mental decision your team must make showing that they are determined to stop their opponents from scoring the next time down the court.

4. We sometimes play a zone defense in half-court in late- or short-clock side out-of-bounds and under-the-basket defensive out-of-bounds situations. Is this a tactic for you to employ?

5. When using an erasable board to diagram plays during a time-out, try to use position numbers or initials so players are not confused and can easily understand their individual assignments. Before the players leave the bench either you or an assistant coach should make sure each player knows his specific assignment as well as the score and number of time-outs you and your opponents have left.

Special Situations You Should Practice Defending

Your players should be aware of time, score, and situation at any time during a game. Setting aside a 10-minute segment in each practice to work on special situations might enable you to win the close games and pave the way to a great season. Here's a list of situations you can practice during that crucial 10 minutes:

1. Two-for-one short-clock opportunities
2. End-of-quarter, end-of-half, and end-of-game plays
3. Following any time-outs (ATO) (Do you want to change defenses?)
4. Crunch plays that teams run when they need a basket
5. Isolation plays
6. Getting the ball out of the primary scorer/ball handler's hands
7. Denying the primary scorer the ball
8. Last-second or short-clock plays with the game in the balance when your team is either tied, ahead, or behind in the score
9. After your team shoots a free throw at the end of the game
10. Situations when you have no time-outs left
11. Inverting and/or switching all late- or short-clock situations
12. Signals and defense to use when your team has a foul to give when not in the bonus situation
13. Knowing which player to foul when you need the ball and must stop the clock at the end of a game
14. Defending plays from different areas of the court at the end of a game
15. Running a particular defense after your team shoots a free throw
16. Jump-ball situations at the end of a game in professional basketball (Uniform rules for professional, college, and high school would help the game!)
17. Special rebounding scheme when opponents might purposely miss a free throw to retain possession of the ball
18. Techniques to stop the clock when time is precious

19. Special defenses that you save for late-clock situations at the end of games
20. Last-minute plays so the players all know their responsibilities if there are no time-outs remaining

How to Stop a Key Player

Stop a star or key offensive opponent by immediately double-teaming him once he receives the ball and

Double-teaming the opponent's star player is one tactic teams have employed successfully. Here the Orlando Magic's double-team of 76ers superstar Allen Iverson forces him into a turnover.
Photo courtesy of NBA Entertainment.

then denying him the ball once he passes out of the double- or triple-team. Don't permit him to get the ball back. Force one of his teammates to beat you if he can.

Free-Throw Alignment

Explain, demonstrate, and practice how you want the players to line up and play on the free-throw line. You should have offensive plays in case of normal missed free throws and also plays for when your team must miss the free throw on purpose. You also need to explain the responsibilities of each player when the opposition shoots a free throw.

How to Line Up. Who lines up next to your opponent's best rebounder? Who pinches the best rebounder from the top, who boxes out the shooter, and who is responsible for boxing out a possible offensive man diving to the goal in case of a missed shot? The answers to these questions will be crucial to winning the game. Your team must be prepared for any and every possibility.

Jump-Ball Alignment

We prefer the three-deep jump-ball defensive alignment in jump-ball situations because we always are concerned with protecting our basket. We do not want to let our opponent score an easy basket off of the jump ball. We always try to tap or channel the ball to the area where two of our players have inside position. If this isn't possible, we may try to tap or influence the ball to a designated corner where our teammates know we might try to tap the ball. We are reluctant to tap the ball back in the direction of our opponent's goal. When we know we have an advantage on the tip, we might screen one of our opponents and look for quick possession and an easy scoring opportunity. We always look to catch the other team's defense napping.

Teams set up their jump-ball alignments in a box set, a diamond, and even a spread set to try to gain control of the opening tip. They constantly probe for the slightest advantage. Your team should too.

Defending Out-of-Bounds Plays

We want our players to play pressure defense on out-of-bounds plays. We always try to take something away from the opponent. Most out-of-bounds plays are set up to enter the ball safely but the opponent's focus might actually be designed to get a quick scoring opportunity. We try to stop the quick scoring thrust and use the shot clock to our advantage. In short-clock situations we may invert and switch every time offensive players cross with or without the ball or simply switch whenever offensive players cross. Our short-clock (under five or seven seconds) defense might be a zone trap where we channel or force the ball to the corner and then aggressively trap the first pass and front or overplay all of the near outlets while leaving the farthest man from the ball free. We tempt the defense to find him while using up valuable time on the shot clock. We want to deny the offense a shot if at all possible in a short clock situation. We prevent all lob passes if possible.

Here are some tips you can use to teach your players how to defend out-of-bounds plays effectively.

1. Side: When we use man-to-man defense on a side out-of-bounds play, if we front the post we want to pressure the inbounds passer and not leave ourselves vulnerable to a lob pass into the post from out of bounds. When we play three-quarter on the post we prefer to pressure the inbounds pass or have the defender on the passer play fake or feint pressure on his opponent.
2. Baseline: The defender on the inbound passer should pressure the ball and also pro-

tect the goal. At times we may even ask him to trap or switch on the ball when it is passed to his immediate outside shoulder.

3. Mid-court: Work with your players on defending all types of alignments and make them aware of how you want to play a pass into the backcourt.

4. Short corners: Do your players know if you want to play man to man, trap, zone, or switch in this situation? How does the shot clock impact these decisions?

5. End-of-game, half, or quarters: How do you want to defend? Explain to your players how time, score, and situation influence your defensive decisions.

6. Full-court inbounds: Explain what you want to happen at the end of the game, beginning of a quarter, and following time-outs or free throws.

7. Inbounding the ball from random spots on the court: What defense do you prefer to play? What are your choices?

8. Short corner out-of-bounds play with five or fewer seconds on the shot clock: How will you play this? Will you use zone or man to man and try to trap and seal the first pass, or will you line up and show zone but actually play man to man, switch everything, and try to stop your opponents from scoring? You may be afraid to trap because you know your opponents realize they have to get a shot off or lose possession of the ball. Why gamble on trapping? This is a decision you as a coach must make. Are you a risk taker? How much confidence do you have in your defense?

9. Two-for-one situation: It is the end of the quarter with more than 24 and less than 36 seconds on the game clock. Your opponent has the ball, but you have a nonshooting foul to give. Do you let the shot clock run

down, foul them before they can get a shot, and then give them the ball on the side and let them run a play for a possible score? Or do you play strong defense, try to stop them from scoring by making them shoot a jump shot, save your foul, and give your team the opportunity for the last shot? The coach must prepare his team to respond to and defend this situation.

Questions a Coach Should Consider

1. When and why do you change defenses and press?
2. What special situations might dictate these changes?
3. Are you losing?
4. Do you want to change the game's tempo?
5. Do you want to stop a particular player?
6. Does your opponent have an offensive flow and rhythm you want to stop?
7. Do you want to try to extend your lead?
8. Do you want your bench to change the game's direction?
9. Are you preparing for a future opponent?
10. Do you want to see how your players adapt to change?

14

Scouting

In the NBA we rely very heavily on scouting our opponents before we play them. Coaches usually view videotape of an upcoming opponent's last three or four games as well as previous games we have played against that team. That may sound excessive, but it is necessary because many teams change plays and strategies depending on the opposing team's defense or personnel. Most professional teams also have a full-time advance scout on the road attending games. Many times he at least scouts our next opponent's previous two games, especially if we have not played them in some time.

Scouting the Opposition

Because we play so many games in the NBA season, we get a chance to see what works and what doesn't. Most coaches believe that if it doesn't work, change it. They also believe in embracing systems that are successful and that is why the triangle offense of the Chicago Bulls and Lakers was copied and why a number of teams are using some of the offensive philosophy of the Sacramento Kings and New Jersey Nets, which were modeled after the Princeton offense. The Princeton offense is motion-oriented and relies on backdoors, flares, and dribble handoffs in addition to opportunities to run for easy baskets in transition. It is more varied than much of the typical NBA game, which consists of isolations, pick and rolls, and post-ups.

When scouting or preparing to play an opponent there are certain things most coaches want to know about the other team:

1. What are a team's offensive tendencies?
2. What types of plays do they run? What do they run in need situations?
3. Who are their best offensive players and rebounders?

4. What plays do they run out of time-outs (ATO)?
5. How do they begin each half?
6. How do they defend the pick and roll, isolations, and the low post?
7. Who are their best and poorest free-throw shooters and their most dangerous three-point shooters?
8. Who are their go-to guys?

In the NBA, advance scouts usually provide their teams with full-fledged reports that consist of a call sheet listing every play the opposition runs and the frequency with which they have run each play in their most recent games as well as diagrams of each play and its options. They also separate the opponent's side out-of-bounds plays, their baseline out-of-bounds plays, plays used immediately following time-outs, plays run following free throws, offense versus zone defense, press offense and defense, crunch or need plays—plus anything else the scout thinks the team should consider in its game preparation.

In addition to this information our scout presents a one- or two-page summary of our opponent's last game, which includes game comments, a depth chart, basic offensive philosophy, basic defensive philosophy, defense versus the post, defense versus the pick and roll, and the scout's thoughts about how we should play this opponent. The scout also outlines the opponent's top offensive sets, their poorest free-throw shooters, their most dangerous three-point shooters, and their best rebounders.

Once the report is received, the assistant coach responsible for preparing the video scouting pregame tape and presenting the report at our shootaround and team meeting has a chance to read the report, he follows it up with a telephone call to the scout to discuss our game plan. We work very closely with our advance scout to ensure we are fully prepared for each opponent.

15

Miscellaneous Drills

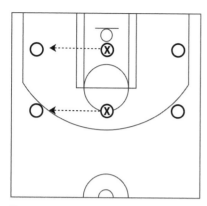

Figure 15.1
First pass: defenders close out.

Figure 15.2
Defenders close out and trace the ball.

This chapter outlines some defensive drills you can use to prepare your team for a winning season.

Defensive Drills

Michael Holton's Close-Out Drill. Michael Holton, head coach at the University of Portland, is responsible for this great drill. The purpose of the close-out drill is to work on closing out on the ball, pivoting, and breaking your body down into a defensive stance. It is important that players close out and stay in a stance while tracing and controlling the basketball. Each defender closes out three or four times (approximately 30 seconds) before rotating to one of the other positions. Each player rotates from defense to offense.

The defenders (X's) start with the ball. On the coach's whistle or command, the X's pass the ball to the offensive players, the O's, and close out (Figure 15.1).

The X's trace (pressure) the ball while the O's, the offensive players, move the ball around faking and simulating passes.

On the coach's whistle, the offensive player (O) passes the ball to the offensive player opposite him.

The X then pivots, runs, and closes out on O and pressures the ball (Figures 15.2, 15.3, and 15.4).

Continuous Three-Against-Two Defensive Fast-Break Drill with a Trailer Stepping in at Mid-Court. We begin by dividing up our squad into two teams in different colored jerseys set up at either side of mid-court. We then number the players on each team in sequence. To begin, the first two players in the X line (X^1 and X^2) go to one basket and set up in a tandem defense, and the first three O line players (O^1, O^2, and O^3) begin behind half-court and attack X^1 and X^2. Meanwhile O^4 and O^5 set up a tandem defense at the far offensive end of the court. Once the O's and the ball cross half-court, X^3 runs in from the sideline, touches the center circle, and then runs toward the basket as a trailer to help X^1 and X^2 defend against the three offensive players. Once the offensive players score, the defenders steal the ball or get an offensive rebound, all three team X players break toward the offensive basket defended in tandem by O^4 and O^5 who have raced up toward the mid-court line. Once the ball has crossed half-court, O^6 runs on the court, touches the mid-court circle, and sprints to help his defensive teammates defend the fast break. The player making the last pass on the fast break goes to the end of his team's line at half-court and the other two offensive players remain on the court to defend against the next group that attacks their basket.

The three defensive players break toward the other basket where two defenders are waiting at mid-court. We then rotate as before with each player following the player in front of him. The first team to score 11 baskets is the winner. We don't worry about fouls, but we will blow the whistle and penalize a team if necessary. This not only teaches fast-break defense, rebounding, and offensive skills, but it is a great physical conditioning drill as well. We have a coach working with the offense and another with the defense. Our defensive emphasis is stopping the ball, rebounding, boxing out, and defending the goal.

Continuous Full-Court Two-Against-One, Three-Against-Two, Four-Against-Three, Five-Against-Four, and Five-Against-Five Fast-Break Drill. We begin by dividing the squad into four teams and placing one team at each hash mark at the sides of the court. Two offensive players with the ball at one free-throw line attack a defender at mid-court in a two-on-one fast break. The lone defender then tries to stop the break. Once he has accomplished this or the offensive players score, he and a wing player from

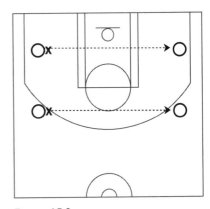
Figure 15.3
Second pass: defenders run on the pass to close out on the other side of the court under control to prevent dribble penetration.

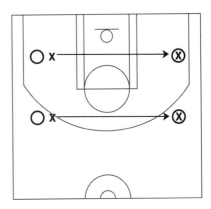
Figure 15.4
Second trace: contest jump shot but stop dribble penetration.

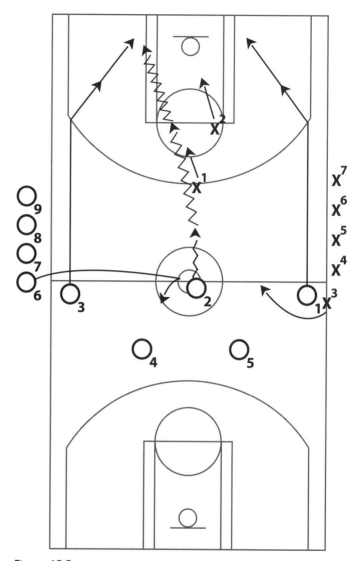

Figure 15.5

The continuous three-on-two fast-break drill with trailer can be played to a winning game of 10 baskets. Once the ball crosses half-court, X^1 runs and touches the mid-court circle and tries to catch up and help X^2 and X^3 play defense. O^2 dribbles ball to the free-throw area and stops and shoots or passes to O^3 or O^1 breaking for layups. X^2 and X^3 try to stop the fast break in a tandem defense setup. Teams get one point after a score or rebound. X^1, X^2, and X^3 break toward the other basket where O^5 and O^6 are in a tandem defense to meet and stop them. Once the ball has passed half-court, O^6 touches mid-court and helps O^4 and O^5 defend and rebound. The offensive player on the break who throws the last pass goes to the end of the line at mid-court, and the other two offensive players play tandem defense.

each corner run a three-man fast break against two defenders who have run up to mid-court from the opposite corners to defend the three-on-two fast break. Again, once the offensive team scores or the defenders steal the ball or get an offensive rebound, the two defenders plus a wing player from each of the nearest hash mark run a four-man offensive transition against three new defensive players stepping in at the other end of the court. Once this four-on-three break is completed or stopped, the three defensive players plus two players coming in from the hash mark run a five-on-four fast break against four defenders at the other end of the court. These five offensive players try to score, but whether they do or do not, the four defenders plus another player stepping in from the hash mark, get the ball as if it were a real game and go five against five toward the opposite basket against the five offensive players who have just scored or lost the ball via a steal or turnover. We continually rotate the players into all positions and try to simulate transition situations (Figure 15.5).

Three-Against-Three-Against-Three or Four Against-Four-Against-Four Continuous Full-Court Drill. Four teams dress in different colored jerseys; two of these teams will be at each basket. We begin by playing four against four at one basket. As soon as one team scores or is stopped, their opponent gets the ball and attacks the next basket where, at mid-court, a team of an equal number of players is waiting to defend them. We run this drill continuously until one team achieves a predetermined number of stops (five or seven). The winners gets water and shoot free throws, and the losers play a three-team round-robin to a predetermined number of stops (three or five). We emphasize full- and half-court organization.

We can set up the type of defense we want to play; double teaming, run and jump, trapping the first wing pass, etc. We can also tell the offense what set or play we want them to run so we can practice defending that maneuver. The drill simulates game situations and is highly competitive. As the coach, you decide on the penalty you assess to the losers or the reward you give to the winners.

Three-Against-Two, Two-Against-One, One-Against-One Continuous Fast-Break Drill. For this drill we have all of our players at one end of the court. We set up a three-on-two fast-break drill going toward the opposite end of the court. Once the offensive team scores or the defenders come up with the ball, the two defenders attack on offense against the previous offensive player farthest from the ball who has now become the defender in a two-on-one situation. At the other end of the court when the offense scores or the defense captures the ball, the defender becomes the new offensive player and attacks the offensive player farthest from the goal who is then a defender in a one-against-one full-court drill.

Defensive Tip: Our defensive objectives in each of our outnumbered defensive full-court drills are to guard the goal, stop the ball, make the offense pick up the ball by faking or feinting, turn the ball over, take a bad shot, or slow the ball up and contain it until our teammates can get back on defense. We constantly emphasize and practice our transition defense as much as possible.

Four-Against-Four Half-Court Drill and Game of Stops with a Coach as the Passer. We play four against four on the half-court beginning with the ball just inside the mid-court line. When the defensive team gets a stop via a turnover, steal, or defensive rebound, they throw an outlet pass to a coach on the sideline. They earn a point for the defensive stop. They then sprint toward mid-court and remain on defense against four new offensive players. Once one member of the offense receives a pass from the coach, it signifies the start of play. If the original defensive team gave up an offensive rebound before they stopped their opponent they earned no points, but they have earned the opportunity to remain on defense. If the offense scores, they become the defense, but earn no point. Teams go from offense to defense only if they score. If they fail to score, they go to the end of the offensive line. Once one of the teams has accumulated seven stops (or a number predetermined by the coach), that team is declared the winner.

16

Summary

It is important to recognize your players' abilities and then formulate your defensive philosophy according to their particular physical attributes and attitudes. Try to identify your initial defensive objectives and goals. Whether or not you decide to play pressure defense on the full or half-court, shrink the half-court, or pack your defense in and make your opponents beat you from outside, you have to be consistent in your defensive planning and strategy. It is a step-by-step process that must rest upon a solid foundation and a systematical approach.

This book was written to provide you with ideas and potential alternatives to ponder and possibly experiment with. You may be of the school that simply believes that outscoring your opponent should be the main objective, with defense as an afterthought. It's true that if you score more than the opposition, you win. But what about those games when your team has a poor shooting night, faces a team that wants to slow the game down and limit possessions by using a full shot clock every time down the floor, or simply has more weapons and superior personnel? Defense can be the great equalizer in the face of these and other challenges you and your team may have to deal with.

Every time I discussed, edited, or reread this manuscript, I thought of other drills or concepts that might have been included. Please use this book as you deem appropriate to your particular situation. Use it only as a guide and never stop seeking to add to your basketball knowledge.

You must work diligently to prepare your players, implement your system, and get them to believe the possibilities are limitless. Building a dominating defense takes a tremendous amount of persistence, concentration, and determination, but I cannot overstate the rewards that will follow.

Getting It Started: The Warm-Up
By Arnie Kander, Strength and Conditioning Coach/Physical Therapist, Detroit Pistons

Warm-Ups

I feel that one of the most crucial areas related to conditioning begins with the warm-up. The warm-up is part of practice, not a separate entity. Over the years I have found that most coaches hate the warm-up part of practice because of its lack of practicality. There are several things that a proper warm-up should include:

1. Specific movements that will be utilized on the court
2. Progression going from basic to more complex movements, and from slow, controlled movements to more up-tempo movements
3. Biomechanically sound work on alignment and core strength
4. Specific running drills that emphasize proper technique and develop awareness of all the movements that will be performed within a game

I feel that spacing is crucial to a proper warm-up, and there should be enough room between each athlete so that the movements can be performed properly. The warm-up is performed entirely standing and at no time are the athletes on the floor "stretching." Floor stretches violate the rules of preparation in that the movements are neither progressive nor specific to the game of basketball. Most athletes cannot perform them in a biomechanically correct way. Whenever an athlete finishes a floor stretch he must then stand up and stretch some more to loosen up from the floor stretches. In addition, most coaches hate the time spent on the floor because it usually involves conversation, lack of focus, or in some cases sleep. The warm-up should mentally prepare the athletes to begin practice, not put them to sleep. I feel that the warm-up sets the tone for the practice. If possible, all coaches should be involved and perform the movement portion of the warm-up. It should be a total team activity.

Starting Position

This is the position in which the athlete begins each movement. Just as the triple-threat position is vital on the court, the starting position is crucial during the warm-up. The feet should be pointed directly forward with weight evenly distributed throughout the foot, the knees slightly flexed, the pelvis in a neutral position so that the back is not too rounded or too arched, the shoulders held strong and not rounded forward, and the eyes straight ahead. The whole principle is to lower your center of gravity and to develop the flexibility, strength, endurance, and body awareness to maintain this alignment throughout the warm-up.

Basic Routine: Six Repetitions of Each Movement

1. Arm swings front to back: Maintain your posture as you slowly allow your arms to swing forward and backward behind your hips. As your arms go behind your hips, your shoulders will try to round, and when your arms go forward at shoulder height your lower back will try to arch. These are compensations made by the body either because of weakness, lack of flexibility, or poor mechanics. Do not allow the compensation to occur.

2. Arm reaches: With your palm facing you, reach one hand at a time toward the ceiling (forward shoulder press) trying to keep your palm facing you the entire way. Keep your elbow in toward

your side during the movement. Alternate arms. If your palm starts to rotate away from you or your elbow shifts from your side (compensation) do not raise any higher than this.

3. Arm reaches across the body: With your palm facing upward, reach your hand across your body allowing your trunk to rotate. Alternate arms. Whichever arm is reaching, the opposite arm should be bent at the elbow, and the elbow should be pulled back behind the body to allow clearance for the reaching arm.

4. Ankle bends: Perform partial squats keeping the back upright and not allowing your upper body to fall forward. The knees should go forward over the toes and not fall inward. The heels remain on the ground. This is a great exercise for lowering your center of gravity. As the ankles become stiffer (players lose up to 30 percent of their ankle flexibility) they bend forward from the hips, which causes them to lose balance, reaction time, and strength generated from their legs.

5. Ankle bends (one step forward): Place your feet at a width just slightly inside the hips. Step forward three to six inches. Perform the ankle bends from #4. Make sure your weight is evenly distributed between your back and front foot. Keep your knees in line over your toes (especially your back foot). You will find that when the feet get behind your hips there is a tendency to turn the feet out or cave the knee in during the movement. This compensation leads to tendonitis, joint irritation, and overall loss of performance. Perform on left and right sides.

6. Leg stride: Continue to move your feet closer together and then step forward so that your feet are approximately three to four feet apart. Your lead knee should be flexed so that it is directly over the toes. The back foot should be

aligned straight with the heel flat on the ground. It will require balance and postural strength to maintain this position. This is your stride. While holding this position raise your arms to your side at shoulder height six times. Then raise to the front six times. You will have to learn to hold the stride position while other muscles are activated. Perform on the left and right sides. This position will lengthen the hip flexors and calves, and place less strain on the hamstrings. If the hip flexors are tight, the hamstrings must work even harder to extend the hips during running that leads to possible injury and reduced performance. In addition, tight calves lead to early heel rise during the push phase of running; therefore you do not get the optimal acceleration that comes from more elastic calf muscles.

7. Cross leg stretch: Cross one leg behind the other. Do not allow your back knee to lock back. With your elbows straight reach your hands straight behind your hips and hold for six seconds. Then reach your hands straight out to your sides and hold for six seconds. Reach straight in front and hold for six seconds. Lean forward keeping your back straight. Go as far forward as you can while still keeping your back straight. Hold for six seconds. Perform on left and right sides.

8. Standing trunk rotation: Go back to your starting position and, with your elbows flexed, rotate your trunk 60 degrees to each side back and forth six times. Your eyes should stay straight ahead and you should begin to feel your abdominal muscles initiate the movement. Your back muscles in addition to your abdominals will help with the change of direction taking place during the movement.

9. Standing trunk rotation with elbows straight: This is the same movement as #8 except that

your arms are straight. The hand should finish right in front of your eye while the other arm is pointed out to the side. Your feet remain flat during the movement, and your eyes continue to face forward.

10. Golf rotation: Perform golfing movement allowing your feet to pivot and your head to move. Perform at a slow, controlled pace. It is important to use your abdominal and back muscles for this movement.

11. Midlevel rotation: With palms facing upward, rotate your trunk across your body while still allowing the feet to pivot during the movement. Your hand should rotate past midline.

12. High-level rotation: Continue to perform the rotation but arc the movement so that your hand reaches up toward the ceiling as you pass midline. As you rotate left, the right hand should be doing the reaching. As you rotate right the left hand will be doing the reaching.

13. Running technique: Perform a running motion while keeping your feet stationary. Your hand should point right in front of your eye on the same side of the body. As you move your arms up and down, each hand alternately comes in front of your eye as you simulate the correct way to move your arms as you run. Your fingers and shoulders should stay relaxed with no feeling of tension. Your opposite arm should reach back with your elbow high toward the ceiling. Try to reach your hand past your hip. Keep your chest up and your vision forward. In order to keep your hand in line with your eye you must use your abdominal muscles to rotate your spine slightly. There will also be a rhythmic bending of the knees matching the upper-body movement.

14. Marching technique knees high: Continue the upper-body movement in the running motion and add a marching motion with your legs.

The left hand and left foot should come forward at the same time. The thigh should come forward so that it is perpendicular to the ground. The alignment should be such that the knee and foot are in line without any rotation.

15. Marching technique knees mid: Continue the upper body motion and marching, but this time focus on bringing your feet directly up behind your buttocks. This will require more flexibility in the knees and will begin to utilize more hamstring activity to produce the movement.

16. Marching technique feet behind: The upper-body movement stops but now the legs continue to march with the feet going behind the body toward the buttocks. This will resemble a reverse leg curl. It is important to keep the knees together and the upper body in good alignment. The chest stays upright with no side-to-side movement. Make sure the foot goes directly behind the body. This requires more knee flexibility and is a great warm-up for the hamstrings.

17. Marching technique cross body: Continue marching, this time crossing the knee across the body. The upper body remains square during the movement. This helps to stretch the lateral hamstrings, gluteals, and hip rotators.

18. Marching technique upper and lower cross: Continue as in #17, but this time as you cross the leg also use the opposite arm and move them across in a reciprocating manner. The right knee and left arm should cross and the left knee and right arm should cross.

Running Preparation

1. Jog in place. Stay light on your feet, using the entire foot. Do not bounce up and down. Learn to absorb the shock from your feet through your ankles, knees, hips, and back.

2. Jog front to back. Go forward five feet; then use your left leg to stop your body and jog backward. When stopping, keep your knees directly over your feet, and keep your back upright so that you do not fall forward. Keep your eyes upright during the movement. Alternate legs so that the next time you go forward you use the opposite leg to push off.

3. Jog with weight shift (side to side): After jogging forward five feet, use your left leg to change direction and shift to your right; then jog backward. Repeat from right to left. The change of direction should only be two to three feet in width. This requires that you bend your knees to maintain balance and have strength in your legs to allow a proper change of direction of movement. The movement should resemble a small rectangle.

4. Jog with weight shift wide: Perform the same as above except make your weight shift wider (four to five feet). Make sure your knees are bent and your body is in a balanced position. Do not lean too far forward or drop your eyes. It is important not to jump from leg to leg; keep your center of gravity level. Hold your arms out wide at shoulder height with hands open when performing the weight shift. Most athletes have a tendency to close their hands or drop their arms during the movement.

5. Carioca: Although you perform this movement to the side, it is different from the traditional football carioca. The feet should never cross during the movement. One foot should line up directly in front of the other during the cross phase of the movement. This requires flexible hips to reduce the amount of torque on the low back. Also, the feet will point directly forward if this technique is stressed. I like to do the drill three different ways, with the hands also moving matching the legs, with the hands pointed directly out to the sides, and with the

hands pointed directly overhead. By doing the last two movements you are learning to stabilize a segment of the body while another segment is moving.

Running Program

The spacing during this phase can be three lines, two lines, or one line (follow the leader). No matter which is chosen it is essential that there is good spacing between each athlete so that proper technique can be maintained. The distance chosen for the running drills can vary but is usually either full court or three-quarter court. The following order of running drills is progressive and will systematically warm up the body.

1. Backward running: Keep the body level, pump your arms during the movement so that your hands go past your hips and then back directly under your eyes. I always start backward because it takes pressure off the knees and back, and it's also a good way to teach bending the knees during the lift phase of running. It requires balance to run backward so you are activating the balance receptors while quieting the pain receptors in the body.
2. Forward running: Keep your eyes level and continue to use your arms in the same manner. Remember this is just a light jog.
3. Backpedal S: Perform the backward jog, but this time do it in a slight S-curve fashion. You should look over your shoulder in the direction you are curving. Therefore, if you are curving right, you should be looking over your right shoulder and vice versa.
4. Forward S running: Perform the forward jog in a slight S curve. This time the head should also curve with the body. The reason for angling the head is that the body will follow the head's alignment.

5. Backpedal skip: This movement primarily occurs at the ankles and the knees do not bend a lot. The movement will loosen the hips and start to add a little vertical load onto the body. Vertical loads put more pressure on the tendons and joints, so we start them out slowly.

6. Forward skip: Same as the backpedal skip in that the knees bend slightly. Keep the arms moving in a rhythmic fashion.

7. Backpedal high-knee skip: This time bring the lifting knee to 90 degrees, with the heel going toward the buttocks. There is no bounding during this movement; it is performed for flexibility and core strength. It requires core strength to keep the upper body in a strong athletic position while the hips and knees are working. Keep your back in alignment. Do not lean forward or backward.

8. Forward high-knee skip: Same as above with the lifting knee coming forward and the thigh parallel to the ground. Once again, there is no bounding during this movement.

9. V cuts: Jog four to five steps on the diagonal and then use the outside foot and change direction. Make sure it is a strong plant. Your head and shoulders change direction prior to the hips turning in one direction. Perform back and forth from the right to the left.

10. Bounding skips: Increase the vertical load by trying to skip six to eight inches off of the ground. Alternate the right and left legs. Use your arms to provide power for the movement. Keep your core strong during the movement. You can use your arms in two different forms including the running motion or the finishing motion. The running motion is the pumping of the arms so that the right arm and left leg come forward together. On the finishing motion the hand goes high as if finishing a layup and the right leg and right hand go for-

ward together. Make sure your arms are strong with good technique for both forms.

11. Change of direction: Run forward to the free-throw line, change to a backpedal until half-court, switch to forward until the opposite free-throw line, and then finish with a backpedal to the end of the court. If you are turning over the right shoulder, then you should lead out with the right leg when going from the backpedal to the forward movement.

12. Change of length: Jog from baseline to the free-throw line, increase stride length from one free-throw line to the other, and finish with a jog to the baseline. Make sure that you do not overstride (if your lead foot lands in front of your knee, you are overstriding). Your foot should land directly over your foot. Also watch the position of your upper body and hands. Keep your upper body strong and your hands pumping by your sides. Your elbows should not leave your sides. Remember that as you increase stride length you will also increase upper-body length so that your hands will reach back past your hips, keeping your elbows high and pointing straight back. Your abdominal muscles produce the rotation of the trunk, which creates tremendous power that is translated from the legs up through the upper body. The abdominals maintain the balance and the proper sequence of movement so that you are able to match the upper and lower body stride length.

13. Change of intensity: Jog from baseline to the free-throw line; then increase speed to 70 percent from free-throw line to free-throw line; then slow down to the baseline. Next time increase the speed to 80 percent and then 90 percent. This allows you time to let the calves and hamstrings fire at a faster speed in addition to utilizing more flexibility in the hips. I

never have athletes warm up at 100 percent speed for reasons of injury prevention, proper technique, and stamina maintenance for the remaining practice time. As basketball involves so much change of direction and velocity, athletes seldom run at 100 percent speed in any one direction during an actual game situation.

Advanced Warm-Up Drills

1. Cone drills: place one cone at the free-throw line, another at half-court, and a third at the other free-throw line. Run toward the first cone. Then shuffle around without crossing your feet, and run toward the next cone, but this time perform the shuffle in the other direction. Finish on the third cone in the original direction. The arms should be active when you are moving around the cone. Pump hard in a sprinting manner to move you toward the next cone. Do not drop your head and eyes when transitioning from the shuffle to the forward run.

2. Cone drills: Same as above except use two cones three feet apart at half-court and two cones six feet apart at the other free-throw line. This time it will require more distance to shuffle around the cones. Keep sound technique with active hands as you work around the cones. This drill can also be performed in a figure-8 pattern through the cones. You can also have a coach stand in front of the cones so that when you run at the cones, the coach can either point in the direction to begin the drill or call out the direction. This adds a reaction component to the drill.

3. Partner cone drills: Two teammates 10 feet apart perform the initial cone drill at the free-

throw line and half-court. After passing half-court one player receives the ball and the other player becomes the defender all the way to the basket. This will force players to work on their footwork.

4. Multiple cone drills: Place four cones across the free-throw line and half-court. Run from the baseline to the first set of cones and then shuffle through the cones so that you go in front of the first cone and behind the last cone. Run to the next line and shuffle in the opposite direction. A variation of this drill is to run on the diagonal after performing the first set of shuffles to get to the next set of cones. You would therefore have to perform on both the left and right sides.

Supplemental Exercises

These are exercises that can be performed before practice and help prepare the body for the specific movements of basketball. They will help with flexibility, strength, balance, and coordination, which in turn will improve overall performance.

1. Leg swings (front to back): The purpose is to loosen the hip flexors and hamstrings and also to work on hip alignment and core strength. This must be performed on a step so that the swinging leg does not touch the ground. The swinging leg should move from front to back without losing the neutral position of the pelvis and upper back. If you swing too high to the front, the lower and upper back will round over; and if you swing too far back, the lower back will over arch. In either case you are losing core strength, which will lead to a loss of power. Swing the leg as high as you can in both directions without losing the position of

the pelvis and upper back. The other compensation to avoid is pointing the foot or knee too far out from the body when the leg is swinging behind the body. Keep the knee and foot pointed as straight forward as possible when performing leg swings. I usually find that those people that have difficulty with the swing phase behind the body are more prone to lower-back and hamstring problems.

2. Leg swings (side to side): On the same step you used in #1, perform a cross leg swing so that the swinging leg crosses the standing leg to both the front and back sides. As the leg swings around, the other leg does not swing far away from the body. The purpose is to keep the swinging leg pointed straight forward as it goes through its movement. Keep the pelvis square and when the leg goes behind the body do not overarch your lower back to allow the leg to clear the other leg. I usually find that those athletes that have lower-back problems or kneecap pain have difficulty swinging one leg behind the other. It is also difficult for them to keep their feet pointed forward during the movement.

3. Step-ups: These should be performed on a step no higher than 10 inches. The purpose is to warm up the knees and promote optimal alignment in the leg that is standing on the step. Do one leg at a time with no more than 15 repetitions. The knee should stay in line with the toes. If an athlete's knee falls inward, I find it usually means he has a tendency toward knee tendonitis. If the knee sways outward away from the foot, there is a risk of cartilage problems in the knee. This simple drill will strengthen the leg and hip muscles and will wake up the receptors in the joints that create proper alignment, which also will lead to improved efficiency and power.

4. Balance board: By standing on a board shaped like a teeter-totter you can help to develop better balance. The knees should be unlocked and the core muscles activated. The arms should be held in an athletic position and maintained in this position while balancing. Do not allow your upper body to move around to assist with the balance. The balance must come from the legs and the core. You can also perform a series of upper-body movements including chest passes, outlet passes, and shooting motions while maintaining balance on the board. The upper-body movement should not be affected by being on the balance board. It is fine for the board not to be perfectly centered during the exercise. As your balance improves, the board will move less during the exercise.

5. Tennis ball sit-ups: The core muscles will be directly involved during this exercise. Lie on a bench with your feet straight up toward the ceiling (if your hamstrings are flexible enough; if not, slightly bend your knees). Perform a crunch movement and reach up with the tennis ball switching it from one hand to the other behind your legs. Return to the starting position between each rep. Perform reps both clockwise and counterclockwise. You can make the drill more advanced by using two balls and eventually three (with two balls in one hand and one ball in the other). It will take more time with the three balls so more core strength will be needed, and coordination of the hands will be required. As your core gets stronger, you will be able to switch the ball higher up behind the legs. This exercise will also increase hamstring flexibility.

6. Wall tosses: Using a solid wall as backing, perform various throwing movements at various distances from the wall. You can also use dif-

ferent balls, including light rubber medicine balls, basketballs, tennis balls, etc. The movements I like to perform are basic and warm up the movements to be used within practice. They include chest passes, outlet passes, one-hand baseball passes, and side rotation passes. I like to start with the light medicine ball and go to the basketball and then finish with the tennis ball. All movements should be performed with proper technique stressing the importance of the core as the source of the power. Keep your knees unlocked and generate your power upward from your legs, through your core, and up to your extremities, which will complete the movement.

Conclusion

I cannot overemphasize the importance of a fundamentally sound warm-up program. Even if you have an injury and are not going to practice, you can perform the warm-up because it provides rehabilitative movements. During the warm-up you also can correct alignment errors before they become ingrained. (If a player does not practice, I will have him stand on the sidelines and practice various parts of the warm-up exercises. It will help him to work on alignment, strength, flexibility, and balance.)

Some players like to perform lifting movements in the weight room before practice. But by performing these warm-up movements after practice instead of before, you can restore the "normal feel" back to the muscles.

Your body will become very familiar with the warm-up exercises. If you perform them on a consistent basis you will notice less soreness and fatigue and fewer injuries. Your overall level of performance will also increase.

I have found that many of the players perform a mini version of this warm-up before they perform any workout or basketball competition (even summer workouts).

If there are specific floor stretches that you like to use, then I recommend that you do them after practice, when it is OK to shut your body down and rest. In the ideal situations, I recommend that athletes walk or ride a stationary bike (with no resistance) for five minutes after practice. This helps eliminate some of the soreness the following day by flushing lactic acid out of the legs.

Remember to keep all of the movements simple, functional, and easy to follow. The importance of a routine cannot be overemphasized. Players will find that these consistent moves not only make a significant difference in the prevention of and recovery from injury, but also improve overall performance.

Glossary of Basketball Terms

Teams use different terms and symbols to describe specific maneuvers in an effort to teach their players their particular terminology and confuse opponents during a game. This glossary will attempt to clarify this by providing different interpretations of a specific tactic or maneuver whenever possible.

Ahead: Action when the ball is passed from the wing to the corner up the court in early offense or in transition from offense to defense.

ATO: Acronym scouts use to diagram an opponent's play *after a time-out.*

ATW: Acronym for *all the way.* Coaches use this to describe running a set play from start to finish; running all of the play's options before attempting a shot. This familiarizes your players with all the play's possibilities and scoring opportunities.

Backpick, rip, step-up, or **blind screen:** Situation in which a player without the ball comes up behind a player with or without the ball and sets a screen from behind. The screen can be vertical or diagonal.

Back or **butt to the baseline:** Defensive position used to guard a post feeder once he has entered the ball. The defender's stance determines how he wants the feeder to cut after he has passed the ball. We want to take away one of the choices a cutter can make.

Ball-you-man: Defensive position in which a player always keeps his body between the man he is guarding and the basketball.

Belly up or **Body up:** Defensive player making body contact with his opponent by forcing the offensive post man with or without the ball up toward the trapping defender to stop him from easily reversing the ball to an open man.

Blast: Two-one-two high-post offensive set. This can also describe the first diagonal cut from high to low post on the strong side offensively.

Blind pig: Situation in which there is a flash post up from the weak-side baseline to the elbow or pinch post when the offensive wing is overplayed. This sets up the wing for a backdoor cut to the basket once the pass is made to the flashing post player. This classic maneuver is used as a pressure release in any area of the court when a man is being overplayed.

Blitz the pick and roll: Situation in which the screener's defender traps the dribbler and stops the ball as the dribbler's defender chases his man and fights over the screen to double-team the dribbler and stop penetration. Teams may call a color or use an acronym to describe this maneuver.

BOB: Acronym scouts use to describe a *baseline out-of-bounds play* (under-the-basket out-of-bounds play).

Box set: Offensive alignment or set where the four offensive players without the basketball are positioned in a box or square, each approximately 15 to 17 feet apart, usually on or above the elbows and boxes.

Brush screen: Maneuver where a cutter without the ball cuts inside and in front of the player with the ball and goes toward the corner, enabling the player with the ball to drive and slash to the basket.

Bump, chuck, body, or **ride:** Defender makes contact with the offensive player without the ball to slow up, stop, influence, or impede his cut. It can be used against screeners and cutters.

Bump or **bump back:** Screen, flare, pop, or come back to the ball after the offensive player has used your screen. Free yourself when your defensive player attempts to help.

Bury: A situation in which a guard passing to a wing cuts in front of the wing to the strong-side corner.

Buttonhook: Football term used to describe a player faking a cross screen, quickly stopping, coming back to the ball, and sealing his defender on his back. Usually occurs in the lane.

Centerfield: Area above the circle or three-point line in the middle of the court in the offensive end where an offensive player is positioned to receive an outlet pass in case his teammates are in trouble and are having difficulty reversing the basketball. This enables the offensive team to have a player back for defensive balance. May also describe the area above the nail on the free-throw line used to provide weak-side defensive help.

Chase: Term used to define the action where the low-post offensive player goes across the lane in the same direction as the dribbler in the pick and roll. It can also describe the action when a player passes the ball across court or out of the double-team and follows his pass to get free for a return pass.

Cherry pick, tighten, or **leak out:** Defender contesting a shot on a jump shooter takes off for the offensive end of the court hoping for an easy basket following a defensive rebound before the shooter can recover. This tactic is also used to distract or disconcert the shooter to break his concentration.

Circle: Having a post man without the ball circle up or down the lane toward the ball to create a passing lane for the offensive post man being doubled by circling the big man's defender. Can also be referred to as curling to establish a passing lane and outlet. This term is also used to describe the action of the second offensive big man in the pick and roll.

Close out: Method by which a player recovers to an offensive player who has received the ball ready to shoot after providing weak-side help or rotating to contest his shot. Defender must close out quickly but under control to limit dribble penetration.

Contact show: Situation in which a player defends against the pick and roll by keeping in contact with the screener as he jumps out to stop the dribbler.

Corner: Term used to describe the spacing of the players in the overloaded offensive set of the triangle offense. It also describes the area of the court where the baseline and sideline come together.

Counter: Action of an offensive player coming up from the baseline or going over an offensive screener to the weak side, utilizing a back screen to free himself from his defender. This action is also referred to as flaring off a back or jam screen.

Cover down: Situation in which a player is beat on the baseline on a straight-line drive and the nearest player on the weak side must slide down and cross the lane to cover the goal and stop the drive.

Coward's press: Full-court press that does not look to trap and pressure the ball but instead tries simply to slow up the offense and use up time on the shot clock. We may incorporate our one-and-done trap philosophy in this tactic.

Crossing: Action in which two offensive players run from one side of the court to the other with or without screening for each another, forcing their defenders to switch or chase them.

Curl: Situation in which an offensive player runs a man off of a screen by a post player above the block just outside the free-throw lane. The offensive player using the screen immediately curls or curves the screen, practically rubbing shoulders with the screener, in an effort to run his defender off of the screen to lose his man or free the screener or himself to receive a pass for a shot.

Deny and overplay: Situation in which the ball-you-man principle is used to guard a player located one pass away from the ball. The defender must keep his body between the man and the ball to deter or discourage the penetrating pass. This forces the opponent back-door or makes him receive the ball farther out on the perimeter.

DHO: Acronym used to describe a *dribble handoff* between two offensive players.

Diagonal cut: Offensive cut by a player from the weak side to the strong side with or without the use of a screen. This is possibly one of the toughest cuts a defensive player has to guard because the cutter tries to cut across his face and in front of him to receive the ball.

Diagonal down screen: Angled down screen usually set from the high post for a player on the opposite low block.

Digging: Situation where the defender shrinks off of his man on the strong side when a post man has the ball. The object is to disconcert the post player and/or cause him to pass the ball back outside.

Direct or drop: A pass from the point guard to an offensive player on or above the elbow who then makes a straight pass to a player posting up on the same side of the court.

Dive: Action where the offensive player with the ball drives right at a teammate's defender when he is being overplayed. This causes the defender to turn his head enabling the offensive player to go backdoor to the basket for an easy layup.

Double-doubles: Successive double screens for players trying to receive the ball in scoring position. They are frequently staggered and difficult to defend. Many come from the blind side, and the second double usually comes as a surprise to the defense.

Double screen: Two-man shoulder-to-shoulder baseline or other two-man screens.

Double-team: Defensive tactic where two defensive players trap or double-team the offensive player with the ball.

Drag: High or wing pick and roll in offensive transition or early offense that catches the defense by surprise and in an awkward defensive position.

Dribble used: Pressuring the big man with the ball on the perimeter to make him a driver. We want to limit his ability to feed the post or reverse the ball. We pressure and play him as if he has already used up his dribble.

Duck in: Offensive move in which the weak-side low post man flashes or steps into and possibly across the near leg of his defender and up toward the ball to receive a pass from the high post or perimeter in scoring position inside the paint or lane. The offensive player tries to seal his defender on his back.

Early offense: Secondary break situation when the fast break is not available but the defense is not yet set.

Elbow area: Spot located parallel or a step above or below and outside the free-throw lane where an offensive player can post-up with his back to the basket. May also be referred to as the *pinch post*. Defensively we try to pressure and deny all passes to this area whenever possible.

Empty or **clear out:** Term used to let a teammate know he is guarding an isolated player and that the lane and side is clear.

EOG: Acronym for an *end-of-game play*.

FC: Acronym for *full court*.

Fist: Signal used on offense and defense to designate a particular play or tactic. For example, it can be the signal for a pick and roll, post-up, or double-stack action offensively. It can be used defensively to signal a trap. Teams can then add *up, down* or *out, right* or *left* to call a particular play.

Fist to palm or **punch:** often used to indicate a direct post-up on the low block.

Flash or **weak-side cut:** Quick, hard cut to the ball from the weak to the strong side of the floor, mainly through the paint area.

Flat: Term used to describe an offensive set where four offensive players without the ball spread out across the baseline on either side of the free-throw lane.

Flex cut: Horizontal baseline cut by an offensive player over or under a post screener, usually away from the ball, to the strong side through the free-throw lane.

This term is also used to describe a particular offensive set.

Floppy: Term many teams use to describe the offensive set that has wings crossing on the baseline off of down screens set by big men in a scissors action.

Full-body show: Term used when a defensive player off the ball gets his entire body in front of a penetrating player with the ball to either stop the ball or force him to pass the ball uphill or across the court.

Get: Offensive term used for describing a player passing the ball to a wing or perimeter player and following his pass to get the ball back. Some NBA teams use this term to describe a side pick and roll.

Go: Term used to describe a dribble drive from one side of the court to the other on a high pick-and-roll maneuver.

G to F: Acronym for a *guard-to-forward* penetrating pass. Usually refers to a pass that moves the ball closer to the basket rather than away from it. Most offenses usually begin with this type of a pass.

G to G: Acronym for *guard-to-guard* pass. Usually refers to a horizontal pass that swings the ball from one side of the court to the other.

Guard-to-guard: Horizontal pass from one player to the other across the court. This pass usually initiates a two-guard front offensive set such as the blast and frequently is used by teams that emulate the Princeton offense or blast set favored by many NBA teams.

Hand check: Defensive act of forcing or controlling and channeling the dribbler or post man in the direction you want him to go, usually when his back is turned. In the NBA, the defender must use his forearm rather than the palm of his hand to avoid being called for a personal foul. Defenders may hand check a post player with the ball if the offensive player is below the free throw-line extended holding or dribbling the basketball with his back to the goal.

Hawk cut: Diagonal cut off of the high-post area from the perimeter on the ball or weak-side to the strong-side post area or to an area between the baseline and the sideline. Example: From above the weak-side elbow to the strong-side post. Named for a cut used by the Atlanta Hawks in the 1970s and 1980s.

HC: Acronym for *half-court*.

Head hunt: Term used to have the screener screen the offensive player's defender to free a particular offensive player to receive the ball.

Help: Defensive term to describe leaving an opponent to stop penetration of a teammate's opponent.

High post: The area from the free-throw line to above the top of the key or three-point line.

Hold: Maneuver where an offensive player makes his cut and instead of clearing out or screening across he maintains position or posts his defender up on the low block.

Horns: Offensive term or signal used to describe a particular offensive play. Teams can use this symbol to describe different plays.

I: Position of the defenders on the weak side. One weak-side defender is on the elbow and the other on the low block or box. The defender on the ball knows his teammates are ready to help and have these spots covered. We can also have an I on the strong side when the ball is on the strong side wing.

Ice or **ISO:** Abbreviation for a *one-on-one isolation play*. This type of play means isolating an offensive player with the ball and his defender by clearing the other offensive players and their defenders away from the ball, which permits the player with the ball to go one against one versus his defender.

Improve position to gain possession: Term used to teach players that it is the responsibility of the player receiving the pass from a teammate being pressured to step out and create a passing lane. We don't want the passer to force the pass to his teammate if no passing angles have been established.

Inside out: Term used to initiate the offense by going inside first to make the defense shrink, collapse, or trap while the offense kicks the ball out to a shooter.

Inverting: Term that describes keeping the big guys in and the perimeter players out by switching defensive positions on the weak side regardless of where their opponents set up.

Jam screen: Back pick or screen set for a player on his defender once he has passed the ball and cut away to flare off of the back screen.

Kickback: Maneuver where a player with the basketball drives toward the middle drawing the defense and then passing back to an open offensive player who can shoot or post the ball to an inside player who has sealed his defender in the lane.

Level with the ball: Situation where a defender's man is trailing the play and the ball is in front of the defender; the defender needs to get back to the ball to stop penetration. We use this term in our full-court, transition, and half-court defenses.

Lift: Situation in which, when posting up in the drop or direct action, the two or three offensive players not involved in the play step out on the perimeter of the weak side of the court above the three-point line where they keep their defenders occupied so they cannot easily help on the post feed.

Lob: Pass to a post man or perimeter player being fronted or overplayed where the offensive player turns and locks and seals his man or fakes high and goes backdoor to receive a pass aimed toward the front of the rim.

Lock and lob: High-low action when the post man is being fronted or aggressively played on his inside shoulder. The post man turns and seals or locks his defender on his back as the wing on the perimeter passes the ball to the rim or to a player above the foul line where a lob pass is thrown to the low-post player from the player at the high post.

Lock and trail: Situation in which a defender guarding a man receiving a down screen on the strong side forces the offensive player to curl the screen by getting on his hip and outside shoulder to ride him, make him curl, and avoid being screened.

Lock in: When a defender guards a good shooter and does not help or rotate off of him in a trapping or doubling-team defense. We refer to this as "marrying" the offensive player. We want to glove or blanket him to deny him the ball.

Loop: Maneuver used to break defensive pressure by having an offensive man without the ball split two defenders laterally to open up a clear side for the dribbler or to provide a throwback option for the dribbler if the two defenders try to trap him. Some teams also call this maneuver a *split*. It is similar to the throwback option when the dribbler in the pick and roll is trapped and looks to pass back to a teammate.

LSG: Acronym for the *last shot in a game.*

LSQ: Acronym for the *last shot in a quarter.*

Marry: Situation in which a defender completely denies a good shooter the basketball. This defender doesn't help his teammates when the man he is guarding is on the strong or ball side of the basketball in a good position to receive and shoot the ball; instead, he gloves or blankets the offensive player.

Midpost: The area outside the lane half way between the foul line and the low block.

Misdirection screen: Usually a back screen or pick set by the offensive player farthest away from the ball for an offensive player nearest to the ball. This screen is often a surprise and difficult to defend. It can be a cross or flare screen.

Mismatch: Situation in which a taller player is being defended by a smaller or weaker player or possibly a player in foul trouble; the offense wants to direct the ball to him to take advantage of the situation.

Misses/Makes: Results of an offensive play or free throw. Many teams fast break or run their early offense or secondary break on misses only, not when their opponents score a basket or make a free throw. Some teams will run after either a miss or a make to cause the defense to hustle back in transition without getting their defense set.

Motion: Structured freelance offensive scheme where five men are passing, cutting, and screening for one another as well as reversing the basketball looking to create easy baskets off of ball movement. All cuts are dictated by reading the defense so the offense can counter the defense's aggressiveness.

Multiple screens: Successive screens set by the offense to free an offensive player trying to receive the ball for a scoring opportunity or to occupy the defense.

Multiply: Action where a team that has just scored a layup or breakaway basket after a steal immediately regroups defensively and pressures full court to create havoc and another immediate scoring opportunity before the offense can recover.

Need/Crunch: A play used by a team when it must have a basket, usually at the end of the game or in a crucial situation. Your scouting report should emphasize this point.

One and done: Act of trying to trap the ball once in a full- or half-court press. Once the pass is made out of the trap or the trap is unsuccessful, the defense sprints back, retreats, and plays its normal defense.

Open: Similar to *motion.* A passing game without a post man, which emphasizes passing and cutting by all players.

Open and through: Defensive technique used to defend the weak-side pin down. The player guarding the screener opens up to enable the player guarding the screener to cut inside and to the ball side of the screen. Big men may also push up and step back and let their teammate guarding the ball go inside at times when defending the dribbler in the pick and roll.

Penetrate and pitch: Action where the dribbler drives toward the goal and, if stopped by another defender, passes to a teammate for an open shot. This is a tactic along with screening on the ball that can be very effective when playing against a zone as well as a man-to-man defense. This type of action can also be referred to as *draw and kick.*

Pick and roll: An on-the-ball screen usually set by a big man on the dribbler's defender. Designed to make the defense switch or help, enabling one of the offensive players involved to have a scoring opportunity before the defense can recover. One of the most difficult offensive plays a defense must learn to guard.

Pick the picker/Screen the screener: Offensive action where a screener setting a screen for one player receives a screen from another teammate, freeing him for a catch-and-shoot scoring opportunity.

Pinch post: Area outside the elbow where a posting player can set up to isolate his defender. May be set on the weak or strong side.

Pin down: Screen from high to low where the high man screens the low man's defender. The screen can be diagonal or vertical.

Pistol: Signal used for a specific play, usually a flare or jam screen by an inside player for a perimeter player who has just passed the ball. It is difficult to defend because it causes the defense to make a quick decision between a big and small defender while an offensive slip may also be used after the back screen is set.

Playing topside: Action where a defender guarding a player receiving a pin-down screen stays attached to his man but instead of forcing him over the screen tries to force him away from the screen and the ball by playing above him and on his outside shoulder from the beginning of the offensive play.

Pop: Action in which an offensive player fakes a cross screen or an inside cut and then pops back toward the ball to receive a pass.

Power or **punch:** Term or signal that the offense uses to pass the ball inside to a player on the low post.

Reverse or **spin dribble:** When a dribbler begins to drive one way and then spins and changes direction and tries to beat his opponent.

Reverse pick and roll: Action in which a perimeter player passes to a big player on the wing or pinch post and then sets an on-the-ball screen on the big man's defender.

Reverse pivot: Catching the ball with your back to the basket and spinning back to the goal, using your inside foot as your pivot foot and quickly turning and facing your opponent as you whip or sweep the ball in front and away from him.

Ride or **Force High:** To bump, body, and force and ride the cutter over the screen away from the basket instead of permitting him to cut, post up, and gain the position he favors.

Rip: Term many teams use to describe a back pick for a lob or post-up opportunity.

Rip blast: An example of a UCLA, hawk, or zipper cut with a return back pick by the cutter to free the shooter or post a big man. The signal for this type of screen is often a raised fist by the screener.

Roll: Action in which the screener dives to the goal, chest to the ball, with the defender on his back after setting a screen with the intention of having the dribbler pass him the ball. If the defense switches, the roll man has mismatch advantage against a smaller defender.

Rotation: Situation where players must scramble and rotate to find their defensive assignments and the opposition's perimeter shooters after the ball has been passed out of the low post following a double team or trap.

Rover: Term some teams use to refer to the designated trapper on the low post. Other teams use this term to refer to baseline cutters behind the zone.

Rub: Action of cutting an offensive player off of a screen from the weak to the strong side of the court. Similar to a slice cut. Cutters try to rub their defenders off of screens.

Run and jump: Situation in which a defender in front of the basketball leaves his man and tries to trap the dribbler from the front to force him to pass the basketball.

Sag, shrink, collapse, or **dig:** Terms for defenders dropping off of their opponents toward the ball to provide positional help or support to the defender guarding the player with the ball.

Scissors or **double stack:** Offensive play that crosses two players, usually wings, off of low-post screeners with the ball at the top of the key or where one player passes to the post and cuts above the post man and another perimeter player cuts off of the first cutter and splits the post. This offensive set can also be referred to as *floppy, twirl,* or *motion.*

Screen across: Screen set by an offensive player nearest the ball for a man parallel to him and away from the ball. Can also be described as a *cross screen, lateral screen, diagonal screen,* or *horizontal screen.* The man away from the ball can also come across the lane and set a back screen on the player nearest the ball (misdirection screen).

Scripting: Situation in which a team runs through its offensive or defensive plays without opposition (five offensive players against zero defenders).

Seal: Term used when an offensive player uses his body to prevent the defensive player from denying him the ball. It's also a defensive term to describe not permitting the trapped or double-teamed player to throw a penetrating pass between two defenders or turn to the weak side—in other words, to trap and seal him and turn him back to his defender.

Shoot the gap: Defensive term used when the player being screened steps inside and slides through or slips the pick to steal the ball or deny the pass on a down screen or pin down.

Short corner: The area on the baseline approximately three feet outside the free-throw lane where teams want a big man to relocate behind the defense when playing against zone defenses or where we want big men to slide to after setting a screen for a curling or driving teammate.

Show/Showing: Faking or feinting at the ball handler to make him slow down or dribble uphill and away from the basket to help his defender contain him.

Shuffle cut: High-to-low cut to the ball from the strong to the weak side after a pass. The cut is usually a diagonal high-to-low cut where the cutter tries to run his defender off of a screen set by a post man to position himself to receive a pass.

Sideline: A defensive tactic where instead of blitzing or trapping a pick and roll, the defense forces the dribbler down toward the sideline and prohibits him from penetrating to the middle of the court.

Single: Solitary baseline screen.

Skip pass: Cross-court pass over the weak-side defense.

Slice: Weak-side flat or diagonal cut from the wing that uses a single or double screen as the ball is passed around the perimeter.

Slippage: Descriptive term to indicate why a play broke down.

Slip the pick (defensive): Moving inside the screener toward the ball on a down screen; not permitting the screener to make contact when he attempts to set a vertical screen.

Slip the pick (offensive): Pick-and-roll action where the screener's defender is above his outside shoulder and close to the ball. The offensive screener recognizes this and immediately dives to the goal looking to receive a quick pass instead of setting the screen.

SOB: Acronym for a *sideline out-of-bounds* play.

Spacing: The optimum distance on the perimeter for establishing passing angles and lanes by having the offensive players 14 to 17 feet apart to make defensive double-teaming and helping difficult.

Spot up/Space out: Areas where shooters set up on the perimeter and establish passing lanes to receive a pass when the ball is on the low post and the defense may be double-teaming or trapping. Optimum spacing is when the offense positions its players 14 to 17 feet apart.

Squeeze, hug, or **go under:** In pick-and-roll defense, a situation in which the defender on the screener "hugs" his man to permit the defender guarding the dribbler to go under the screener and his defender. This maneuver is often used when the screen is being set outside of the three-point line or when the dribbler is not a good long-range jump shooter. The squeeze can also be used to combat a screen off of the ball to enable the defender to go under both the screener and his defender. Once a repick occurs, some teams automatically trap the dribbler.

Staggered screens: Double or triple screens for a shooter; not shoulder to shoulder but successive.

Step back: On a screen or pick and roll, a situation in which the screener steps back once the dribbler has passed instead of rolling to the goal. This also describes the offensive move where a shooter dribbles into his defender and then quickly steps back to shoot the ball before the defender can close out.

Step in: Action where an offensive player sets a screen and then steps or flares to the ball or where a post player steps into the lane, seals his defender, and looks for a pass from a teammate.

Step-up screen: The action where a player comes up from the baseline area to back pick a player defending the dribbler. This screen sets up an action similar to the pick and roll. It can also be used in the middle of the court as well, in transition or in your early offense if the dribbler is being pressured. Many teams use the step-up screen in two-for-one or short-clock game situations.

Stop: Term used to describe the possession when a defensive team prohibits the opponent from scoring. A team must work to get a stop especially in late-game situations.

Stretch or string out: An attempt by a dribbler being blitzed (trapped or double-teamed) in a pick and roll to try to dribble out to the other side of the court, forcing the high trap man to follow him.

Strong side: The side of the floor where the ball is located.

Swing: Passing the ball from one side of the court to the other through centerfield or the high-post area. This is also referred to as reversing or changing sides with the ball.

Switch: On defense, a situation in which offensive players cross with or without the ball, the two defenders come together to switch assignments and take each other's man. On a switch, the purpose is always to take something away from the offense.

Tandem: Description of the defensive alignment in a fast-break transition three-on-two situation where one player is in front of the other in a straight line from the basket. It is also our defensive alignment for defending some double shoulder-to-shoulder screens.

Three-step-away principle: The distance between a defender and the ball. The distance and the defender's quickness determine if he should attack and trap the ball. If he is farther than three steps away it is probably too large a distance to cover unless he has great quickness and anticipation.

Trailer: In a fast break, the last offensive player into the front court. The fifth offensive player in the fast break is the centerfielder. He is responsible for maintaining defensive balance for his team as he trails the play.

Throw back: Dribbling and penetrating from one side to the other, moving the defense and then passing back to the weak side to a teammate who has screened or looped to facilitate a pass to a player posting up on the low block.

Thru: Offensive term to describe a guard passing to a wing on the same side and cutting away to the weak side of the court to initiate getting the ball from one side of the court to the other.

Thumb: Verbal or hand motion used to signal a particular offensive play.

Top of the head: Hand signal used to designate a particular offensive or defensive play or tactic.

Trap: Action in which two defenders double-team the man with the ball in any area of the court.

Triangle: Term used to describe a play with three offensive players in a pick-the-picker configuration. Also used to describe the defensive alignment in a triangle-and-two combination zone defense.

Turnout/Turn: Running an offensive player from the baseline off a screen or pick usually set by a low-post player so that he can lose his defender and receive a pass in shooting range.

Twirl: Hand signal used to describe a particular offensive action.

Two-for-one: Offensive team's desire to get a quick shot and score with between 30 and 40 seconds remaining in an NBA quarter (24-second shot clock) or half to ensure itself two scoring opportunities to the opposition's one.

Two-man game: Offensive pick and roll, step-up, pinch post, drop, or other play involving two offensive players who are isolated from the other players on the court.

UCLA cut: A passer's vertical cut from the top of the high post to the baseline following his pass to the wing on the ball side.

Up-block: A back screen or back pick between two offensive players without the ball where the lower offensive player screens the defender of the higher player.

Up the line: Action where defenders switch off the men they are guarding and up to the next man when defending a multiple or staggered screen. Again, the objective of any switch is to take something away from the offense.

Utah cut: The opposite of the *hawk cut* whereby a baseline offensive player on the ball side sets a diagonal back screen for a high post man or receives a diagonal down screen from the post player. Named after the Utah Jazz, who frequently used this type of offensive maneuver with John Stockton and Karl Malone.

V cut: Offensive move that describes a set-up step or hard cut in one direction to cause the defender to move away from the area where the offensive player wants to cut. Once the defender leans, the offensive player executes an inside or backdoor cut to get by him.

Weak side: The area of the floor opposite and away from the ball.

Wing: The offensive player on either sideline below or in front of the point man. Most offenses are initiated with a penetrating point-to-wing pass in the foul line extended area.

Zipper: Offensive term to describe a player on the baseline outside the free-throw lane waiting for a vertical down screen from a player on the high post and then using the screen to come high to the ball when the ball is on the wing.

Index

About the Author

Herb Brown brings more than 40 years of basketball experience to the writing of this book. Herb is the older brother of Detroit Pistons head coach Larry Brown. Herb is currently an assistant coach for the Atlanta Hawks.

He served as an assistant on the Pistons' bench during their 2003–2004 NBA championship season. Brown's Detroit history is well documented. He served as the club's head coach from 1976 to 1978 and coached against Larry's Denver Nuggets on six occasions during that time. He led the Pistons to two playoff appearances (1976 and 1977), the club's only back-to-back playoff appearances prior to the Chuck Daly era that began in 1983. Brown's 1976 squad was the only team to advance past the first round of the playoffs prior to Daly's arrival.

A 1957 graduate of the University of Vermont, Brown began his college coaching career at C. W. Post College as an assistant coach from 1960 to 1964. His first head coaching experience was at SUNY Stony Brook (1964–1969), where, in 1969, he was named Coach of the Year after directing Stony Brook to the Knickerbocker league championships.

Brown also has extensive international experience; he led the Israel Sabres—a team consisting of, among other American professional players, former Boston Celtics head coach and player M. L. Carr, former Atlanta head coach Lon Kruger, and former UT–Chattanooga coach Henry Dickerson—to the championship of the European Professional Basketball League in 1975. He coached in the Puerto Rico Professional Basketball League for 15 summers, with his teams appearing in the playoffs each year but one, winning a league champi-

Courtesy: Scott Cunningham/Atlanta Hawks.

onship in 1984 with Canovanas. In 1972, Brown worked under the auspices of the U.S. State Department as a visiting head coach with the Pakistani National Team. He also coached professionally in Spain for six seasons, taking his teams to the playoffs five times, and coached Team USA to a gold and bronze medal in the Maccabiah Games in Israel. He is also on the board of directors of the United States Sports for Israel.

Brown has served as an assistant coach with the Portland Trail Blazers, Houston Rockets, Phoenix Suns, Indiana Pacers, Chicago Bulls, and Philadelphia 76ers. He also served as an advance scout with the Milwaukee Bucks, Pacers, 76ers, and Bulls, earning championship rings in 1992 and 1993 with Chicago. He coached in the CBA for five years, where he won two division championships, reached the playoffs four times, and was the Coach of the Year in 1984. In the WBA, his Tucson Gunners won both the league and playoff championships, and he was also named Coach of the Year.

The six-time Coach of the Year is the author of two other books, *Basketball's Box Offense* and *Basketball Coaches' Guide: Preparing for Special Situations*, and numerous articles that have been published in the United States, Europe, and South America.

Brown, a 2002 honoree of the Hank Greenberg Sportsmanship Award, now resides in Atlanta, Georgia, and Neskowin, Oregon, with his wife, Sherri. He has two married children and four grandchildren.